Conscientious Objectors of the First World War

Conscientious Objectors of the First World War

A Determined Resistance

Ann Kramer

PEN & SWORD
HISTORY

First published in Great Britain in 2014 by
Pen & Sword Social History
an imprint of
Pen & Sword Books Ltd
47 Church Street
Barnsley
South Yorkshire
S70 2AS

Hardback 978 1 84468 119 8

Typeset in 11pt Ehrhardt by
Mac Style, Bridlington, E. Yorkshire

Printed and bound in the UK by CPI Group (UK) Ltd, Croydon, CRO 4YY

Pen & Sword Books Ltd incorporates the imprints of Pen & Sword
Archaeology, Atlas, Aviation, Battleground, Discovery, Family History,
History, Maritime, Military, Naval, Politics, Railways, Select, Social
History, Transport, True Crime, and Claymore Press, Frontline Books,
Leo Cooper, Praetorian Press, Remember When, Seaforth Publishing
and Wharncliffe.

For a complete list of Pen & Sword titles please contact
PEN & SWORD BOOKS LIMITED
47 Church Street, Barnsley, South Yorkshire, S70 2AS, England
E-mail: enquiries@pen-and-sword.co.uk
Website: www.pen-and-sword.co.uk

Contents

Acknowledgements

Thanks are due to the following:

Angharad Tomos for allowing me to interview her about her grandfather David Thomas

Bangor University for access to documents relating to David Thomas

Bexhill Museum for access to archive material relating to Henry Sargent

Felicia Shanahan for permission to reproduce material and images on Richard Porteous.

Harper Collins Publisher for help in regards to copyright for *On Two Fronts*, Corder Catchpool and *Conscription and Conscience*, John W. Graham. The publishers have made every effort to trace the authors, his estate and his agent without success and would be interested to hear from anyone who is able to provide them with this information

Independent Labour Publications (ILP) for permission to take quotes from Fenner Brockway's *Inside the Left*

Library of the Religious Society of Friends in Britain for their help and access to their archives, John Brocklesby's memoirs and the *Winchester Whisperer*

Margaret Sargent for permission to reproduce drawings and photographs by Henry Sargent

Mary Brocklesby for permission to reproduce two photographs of her husband, John Brocklesby

Naomi Rumball for permission to reproduce images from Cyril Heasman's album

Peace Pledge Union (PPU) for permission to reproduce images

Every attempt has been made to contact the copyright holders of quoted materials. Should any references have been omitted, please supply details to the publisher, who will endeavour to correct the information in subsequent editions.

List of Abbreviations

CO	Conscientious Objector
FAU	Friends Ambulance Unit
FoR	Fellowship of Reconciliation
ILP	Independent Labour Party
IWM	Imperial War Museum
NCC	Non-Combatant Corps
N-CF	No-Conscription Fellowship
RAMC	Royal Army Medical Corps
UDC	Union of Democratic Control

Introduction

'We reaffirm our determined resistance to all that is established by the Act'

In 1916 a new phrase – 'conchies' – entered the English language. Used derogatively by press and public, the term referred to conscientious objectors, those men who for reasons of conscience refused to be conscripted and to pick up arms to kill their fellow men. Interestingly, quite a few conscientious objectors, possibly slightly self-mockingly, also described themselves as conchies.

Some 16,000 men took their stand as conscientious objectors during the First World War, or at least from 1916 when, in the face of mounting and horrendous casualties in the trenches, conscription was introduced into Britain. They did so for various reasons: some were motivated by their religious beliefs, others for political or humanitarian reasons, but all believed that it was wrong to accept conscription and profoundly wrong to kill. To say the very least, their stand was not popular. They were mocked and vilified by press and public, were ostracised by friends and family, sacked from jobs, imprisoned and physically brutalised. To most people they were seen as shirkers, cowards and even traitors and they were treated accordingly. Although the Military Service Act of 1916 made allowance for conscience objection, those who took that stand were usually rejected by the tribunals set up to test their sincerity, and handed over to the army, where brutality and abuse were often the norm. In an attempt to break their resistance, some conscientious objectors were even sent to France and threatened with the death sentence. But even this did not shake the resolve of conscientious objectors. Refusing to accept military orders, they were court-martialled and sent to prison, where hundreds endured long prison sentences with hard labour, including periods of solitary confinement on a punishment diet of bread and water. Under the so-called 'cat and mouse' procedure, hundreds were returned again and again to prison. Not all conscientious objectors took such an absolutist stand: some accepted alternative service and a few, mainly Quakers, worked with the Friends Ambulance Service, helping wounded soldiers of both sides.

Despite all the bullying, intimidation and brutality directed at conscientious objectors, nearly all of them refused to abandon their principles and give in: they maintained their resistance right through to the end of the war and beyond, believing as they did that a man's conscience takes priority over the demands of the State, no matter what the consequences. Theirs is a thrilling and inspirational story and, not surprisingly, their actions baffled representatives of the State in the army and in government.

As populations mark the hundredth anniversary of the start of the First World War, much of the attention is focused on the courageous young men who died in the trenches or those who worked on the home front but very little attention is usually paid to those men who, in the face of enormous pressure, had the courage to stand by their principles and refuse to fight. Theirs was a very determined resistance and, in contrast to the many memorials to soldiers who died in the First World War, there are hardly any memorials marking the courage and determination of the men who not only endured considerable hardship to make a conscientious stand but also died or suffered mental breakdown as a result.

Having been part of the anti-war movement since my teens, I feel it is important to try and redress the balance by telling the stories of those remarkable men who held out against the war machine of the First World War to stand as conscientious objectors. Although they were relatively few in number, their impact was far greater than might have seemed: they proved it was possible to use passive resistance to challenge the State, kept the principles of pacifism and a belief in the Brotherhood of Man alive at a time when killing was legion, and paved the way for an influential peace movement that sprang up between the two world wars and still continues today. Their bravery and determination made it possible for the next generation to take their stand as conscientious objectors between 1939 and 1945, helping to inspire not just those second-generation conscientious objectors but also war resisters ever since.

In this book I have concentrated on the British CO movement, which deserves wider recognition. I must though mention that Britain was not the only country where conscientious objectors existed, although the movement was largest in Britain. There were also conscientious objectors elsewhere – in the United States, Canada and New Zealand. Many of them experienced dreadful brutality and discrimination as well.

I owe a debt of gratitude to many people: Bill Hetherington of the Peace Pledge Union who has kindly answered my numerous queries; Naomi Rumball who told me about her grandfather Cyril Heasman, and allowed me access to his precious album of photographs, newspaper cuttings and other items of CO interest – truly a wonderful family heirloom; Angharad Tomas, who told me about her grandfather David Thomas, who paved the way for the Labour Party in North Wales before standing as a conscientious objector, Margaret Sargent and Bexhill Museum who shared knowledge and memorabilia relating to Henry Sargent, respected curator of Bexhill Museum, who served time in Dartmoor for being a conscientious objector, and Felicia Shanahan, who allowed me access to information about her uncle, Richard Porteous. My thanks also to Mary Brocklesby, daughter of conscientious objector John Brocklesby, who was one of the men sent to France and threatened with the death sentence for being a conscientious objector, who kindly gave me permission to reproduce two photographs of her father and my thanks also to the Society of Friends Library in London, where I was able to read John Brocklesby's memoirs, 'Escape from Paganism', and browse through the wonderful *Winchester Whisperer*. I also owe thanks to Peter A.J. Brown, friend of Fred Murfin, who produced and sent me a copy of the original typescript of Fred's story, 'Prisoners for Peace'. Thanks also to Pen & Sword who enthusiastically accepted my suggestion to produce this book. Finally, also my grateful thanks to my friends and partner Marcus, who have given me so much support while I have been writing this book.

Chapter 1

War Begins

'The war of 1914–1918 came very suddenly … I was speaking at Oldham … the next Sunday the guns were firing.'

Fenner Brockway

Deliberate policy or tragic accident, one way or another, on 4 August 1914, Britain declared that the country was at war with Germany, which had that day marched into neutral Belgium. The First World War had begun, the first major conflict to be fought on European soil for nearly a hundred years and the world's first global conflict. At its start very few people could have foreseen what the nature of the war would be and just how many young men would die in the horrors of the trenches. Contrary to popular belief, which claimed that the war would be over by Christmas, the conflict and accompanying bloodbath would continue for four terrible years. As the death toll mounted – worldwide more than more than 30 million men were killed, wounded or declared missing – soldiers on both sides sheltering in the trenches came to believe it would never end.

In August 1914 the British public were not really prepared for war. Although most people were probably aware that that on 28 June 1914 a Serbian nationalist had assassinated Archduke Franz Ferdinand and this had caused turmoil in the Balkans, very few anticipated that within a few weeks there would be war. For most people Serbia was just a distant place of very little interest and there was no reason why Britain should be involved. Towards the end of July, however, the British government realised that problems were developing in Europe. On 23 July Austria-Hungary had delivered an ultimatum to Serbia, followed five days later by a declaration of war against Serbia. Russian forces mobilised in defence of Serbia and the situation escalated. On 1 August Germany, Austria-Hungary's ally, declared war on Russia and issued an ultimatum to Belgium demanding passage through that neutral country; two days later Germany declared war on France and invaded Belgium. Britain, allied to France and bound by treaty to support Belgium, issued an ultimatum to Germany, which expired at 11pm on 4 August. Shortly after a royal proclamation declared that a state of war existed between Britain and Germany.

Right up to the beginning of August, there had been little popular enthusiasm for war. Editorials and articles in some newspapers, notably the *Manchester Guardian*, urged the government to remain neutral. On 1 August 1914 the *Manchester Guardian* wrote that public opinion was 'shocked and alarmed' at the thought that Britain could be dragged into 'the horrors of a general European war', particularly given that Prime Minister Asquith and Foreign Secretary Sir Edward Grey had only the day before stated that there were no treaty obligations on Britain to do so. Big business argued too that intervention in a European war would be disastrous for the economy and a 'disgraceful failure of British statecraft'. By contrast, other newspapers, among them *The Times*, vigorously called on the government to go to war in of support of Russia and France.

The British government too had been divided over the question of war. In 1914 the likelihood of civil war in Ireland, trade-union agitation and the exploits of the suffragettes were of far greater concern to the government than the problems of Serbia. However, as the European situation deteriorated, and although Prime Minister Asquith agonised over the decision, Britain entered the war partly because of existing treaties but also to prevent Germany from threatening national security and upsetting the balance of power. With the invasion of Belgium and subsequent declaration of war, British public opinion by and large swung behind the government and what has been described as 'war fever' gripped the country.

Enthusiasm and opposition

On the day war was declared, huge crowds gathered in central London, jamming the streets around Whitehall and packing Trafalgar Square, while they waited for news. According to *The Times*, the streets were 'packed with cheering masses ... Flags were waved from cabs, omnibuses, and private cars. The plinth of the Nelson Column, the pedestals of the statues in Whitehall, the windows of Government offices served as grandstands … the glimpse of a khaki tunic was the signal for fresh outbursts of enthusiasm …' According to the same account, as the evening drew on and it was clear Germany had not accepted Britain's ultimatum so that the country was now at war, the crowds, on the stroke of midnight, started cheering and singing the National Anthem.

Newspaper accounts of that day stressed the enthusiasm and patriotism of the crowds but just two days earlier central London had been witness to another large gathering, though for quite a different reason. On 2 August 1914 several thousand people had gathered in and around Trafalgar Square for a massive anti-war rally. Photographs of the time show Keir Hardie, the inspirational socialist and pacifist, standing at the foot of the famous lions addressing a huge crowd. Among that crowd was a young man called Harold Bing, who had walked 11 miles from Croydon to be there:

My attitude towards the war was of course critical from the start. This was very largely because I had grown up in a pacifist home. My father as a young man had been very much influenced by his reading of Tolstoy, had become a pacifist and opposed the Boer War and many of the friends who he met and who came to our home were people who took that point of view … when war did loom in the July of 1914 naturally I hoped that this country would not be involved. When I heard that a big anti-war demonstration was to be held in Trafalgar Square on the Sunday 2nd August 1914 and Keir Hardie was to be one of the speakers, I walked from my home up to Trafalgar Square, about 11 miles, and took part in that demonstration, listened to Keir Hardie, and of course walked home again afterwards, which perhaps showed a certain amount of boyish enthusiasm for the anti-war cause which was quite a thrilling meeting with about 10,000 people there and certainly very definitely anti-war though of course at that very same time, while we were demonstrating in Trafalgar Square, the Cabinet was sitting in Downing Street discussing the entry of England into the war and deciding on the ultimatum which brought us into the war two days later on the 4th August …

Harold Bing, aged only 18, would take his stand as a conscientious objector two years later, in 1916. He would be one of around 16,000 men who, for reasons of conscience, would refuse to accept conscription and engage in combat.

Anti-war traditions
Keir Hardie was speaking out against the First World War and was well known nationally and internationally for his long and staunchly anti-war stand, a position that influenced many younger men, encouraging some to become conscientious objectors during the war. But over the previous century there had been a number of pacifist and anti-militaristic voices and societies in Britain, North America and, from the late nineteenth century, in Europe as well. They included religious groups, social reformers and activists in the international socialist movement.

Some religious groups incorporated pacifism as part of their fundamental beliefs. The Society of Friends, or Quakers, was particularly well known for its pacifist standpoint, which dated back to the 1661 Peace Testimony. Although some Quakers both in America and Britain had, at times, taken part in combat, most were pacifists and during the First World War took a leading role in opposing war and conscription. The International Bible Students Association, later the Jehovah's Witnesses, though not pacifist was notable for its refusal to engage in national and international wars and was absolutely opposed to conscription, for which its members were frequently persecuted. Christadelphians also were a large non-combatant religious sect.

In Britain there had been an organised peace movement – albeit very small – that dated back to the end of the Napoleonic Wars. The Society for the Promotion of Permanent and Universal Peace, subsequently known as the Peace Society or the London Peace Society, was formed in 1816. Its members, who over the years included some of the leading social reformers of the day such as free trader Richard Cobden and abolitionist Joseph Sturge, advocated arbitration for resolving potential conflicts, the simultaneous and proportional disarmament of all countries and the setting up of an international authority, tribunal or congress – to some extent foreshadowing the League of Nations, which was formed in 1919. At its height the Peace Society had a membership of around 1,500 and promoted its views through conferences, pamphlets and public meetings. It also had links to similar societies in America. Its roots lay in Christian pacifism and the rationalism of the Enlightenment and many of its members were Quakers. Despite being small by today's standards, the Peace Society was remarkably long-lived and continued until 1930, when it merged with the International Christian Peace Fellowship and soon after ceased to exist.

The late nineteenth century had seen the emergence of a powerful socialist movement, linked to the labour or working class movement that was strongly anti-militarist. Not all socialists embraced pacifism – the absolute rejection of violence – believing as they did in a continuing class struggle that might well involve taking up arms against the ruling class but equally they laid emphasis on the worldwide brotherhood of the working classes. Capitalists and the upper classes created wars; working people were cannon fodder and should resist a situation where the workers of one country were forced to fight their working class comrades in another.

The question of war and militarism was discussed at various international congresses following the formation of the First International (International Workingmen's Association) in 1864. However, delegates were rarely able to agree on a strategy for preventing war, although the most frequent suggestion was that of the general strike. In 1868 the Brussels Congress passed a resolution stating that working men's associations in all the respective countries, working class societies and workers' groups should 'take the most vigorous action to prevent a war between their peoples ...' on the grounds that it would be 'a struggle between brothers and citizens' and urging workers to strike should war break out in any of their countries. However, when the Franco-Prussian War broke out in 1870 neither German nor French workers' movements made any attempt at a strike.

In 1899 the Second International was formed in Paris. An escalating arms race and shifting European alliances meant that the question of war and how it could be prevented assumed greater importance for the socialists and labour groups attending the congresses. In 1891 delegates meeting in Brussels discussed the possibility of a European war and urged labour organisations to 'resist vigorously'. In 1893 at Zurich, Congress urged workers to fight for a reversal of the arms race and for disarmament. War continued to be discussed but agreement was not reached. At the 1907 Congress, divisions were clear: French socialists led by Jean Jaurès argued that socialists should oppose any aggressor; Germans argued that socialists should be prepared to support wars of liberation, such as siding with Russian workers against Czarist oppression – foreshadowing the dilemma for anti-war activists during the Spanish Civil War – and French syndicalists called on workers to stage general strikes and insurrections.

In the event, the final resolution stated that if war threatened to break out, it was the duty of the 'working class and of its Parliamentary representatives in the country involved 'to exert every effort to prevent the outbreak of war by means they consider most effective …'. And if war broke out, the workers should 'intervene in favour of its speedy termination', as well as rousing the peoples to 'hasten the abolition of capitalist class rule'. Keir Hardie for the Independent Labour Party (ILP) and French socialist and pacifist Edouard Vaillant consistently argued for a general strike against war, although once war broke out Vaillant, a lifelong pacifist, like many others supported the French government.

Trying to prevent war
In the month leading up to the outbreak of war, anti-war demonstrations took place in Britain and across Europe. On 25 July 1914, the day that Austria delivered its ultimatum to Serbia, Austrian socialist members of the Austrian parliament published an anti-war manifesto. Over the next few days, German socialists held anti-war demonstrations in Berlin, the French and German sections of the International protested against the war, as did the British Socialist Party. At a meeting of international socialists in Brussels, delegates pledged to demonstrate and lobby against war, while Keir Hardie, Jean Jaurès and others addressed a crowd of some 6,000 Belgian socialists, declaring a 'war on war'. During the last week of July 1914 socialists in France, Germany and Belgium organised street protests, issued manifestos and anti-war demonstrations but, even before the war actually began, it was clear that their protests would have little impact. And in France, the anti-war protest suffered a serious blow when Jaurès was assassinated by a pro-war patriot.

When war actually arrived, there was a surge of patriotic nationalism in all the belligerent nations, as the public swung behind their governments. The European socialist movement was shattered by the coming of war; in France and Germany most socialists acknowledged their failure to prevent war and, in the interests of national unity, gave their support to what many described as a 'defensive' war for survival, particularly in France. Courageously some German socialists, among them Rosa Luxemburg, Clara Zetkin and Karl Liebknecht maintained their anti-war stand but they were in a small minority. The reality was, as Keir Hardie later concluded, international socialism had failed to stop the war.

In Britain the ILP, originally formed in 1893 and led by Keir Hardie, Scottish socialist, pacifist and champion of working people, consistently stood out against war, bringing many supporters into the campaign. One who came under Hardie's influence was Fenner Brockway, who would serve time in prison as a conscientious objector.

The son of missionary parents, Brockway described himself as a rebel from childhood. By the age of 14 he had developed a keen interest in politics and subsequently joined the Liberal Party. After leaving school he became a journalist and was sent to interview Hardie. Armed with note-pad and pencil, Brockway began to ask questions but after a while Hardie told him to put his paper and pencil away and listen. According to Brockway, Hardie spoke for an hour about his own life and the creation of the ILP. The impact on the young journalist was enormous and he remained a socialist for the rest of his life:

> I joined the ILP and was very much under the influence of Keir Hardie … also the whole ILP was anti-militarist, internationalist, we could never think in terms of taking up arms against our fellow workers and, as the war … approached, we became very strongly against the danger of war. Keir Hardie went to international working-class conferences, urged a general strike by all the workers of Europe against the war …

The Labour Party, initially formed as the Labour Representation Committee in 1900, saw its main purpose as looking after the interests of working people, and was more ambivalent in its attitude to war. Even so, there were many anti-war voices not just within the Labour Party but also among the Liberals. From 1911 Labour and ILP MPs, notably Philip Snowden, MP for Blackburn, and Ramsay MacDonald, leader of the Labour Party, attacked Liberal Foreign Secretary Sir Edward Grey for policies that they claimed would lead directly to war. In 1912 the Labour Party Conference supported a motion from Keir Hardie, protesting against the Liberal government's anti-German policy. In the two years leading up to the war the ILP highlighted and campaigned against the growing arms industry. As late as 30 July 1914 the Parliamentary Labour Party stated their hope that 'on no account will this country be dragged into the European conflict ...' and urged labour organisations to take 'effective action' to oppose war.

Liberal and socialist newspapers such as the *Daily Herald* and the *Daily Express* called for mass demonstrations, while on 30 July 1914 the ILP's own newspaper, the strongly anti-war *Labour Leader*, included an editorial by Fenner Brockway, who was by now editor of the paper, headed 'The War Must be Stopped – and We Must Stop It'. Within his editorial, Brockway, who would soon be a major activist in the no-conscription and conscientious objector movement, argued that if the European labour movement worked together war would be impossible: 'No Socialist conscience would approve the war which is looming before us if it came upon us. We have the power to stop it. We must do so. How? By demonstrating in such numbers and with such fervour all over Europe that the various Governments will be made to realise and fear the strength of the anti-war party ...'

Plans were made for massive demonstrations to take place on 2 August. The ILP urged the largest of its branches to take action and organise anti-war meetings in their localities; in Scotland, James Maxton, chairman of the Scottish ILP, estimated that more than 100 meetings had taken place throughout Scotland. Largest of all the demonstrations was the one held in London's Trafalgar Square, where an estimated 15,000, including Harold Bing, gathered to hear Keir Hardie, George Lansbury, Will Thorne and others speak out against war. The crowds listened to speeches, waved red flags and banners and sang 'The Red Flag' and 'The International'. Possibly as many as 100,000 socialists and Labour supporters demonstrated across Britain on 2 August, but in reality they were in a very small minority.

The following day, 3 August, Sir Edward Grey announced in the House of Commons that Britain's commitment to France meant war was a matter of 'national honour'. The Conservatives, under Bonar Law, pledged support for the Liberal government, as did the Irish Nationalists. There were three senior members of the government who opposed the war – Charles Trevelyan, Parliamentary Secretary of the Board of Education, John Burns, President of the Local Government Board, and John Morley, Secretary of State for India – and they resigned in protest. Others, among them Philip Snowden, voted against the decision, while Ramsay MacDonald, leader of the Labour Party, told the House of Commons that the decision was wrong, arguing that Britain should remain neutral, a stand that brought him considerable abuse from the public. Despite the opposition, the motion for war was carried and on 4 August, Britain declared war on Germany. Soon afterwards, the Parliamentary Labour Party also moved to support the war. MacDonald resigned in protest, his place being taken by pro-war Arthur Henderson.

For Keir Hardie, who had campaigned so intensely to prevent war, its arrival was devastating. Writing in the *Labour Leader* on 6 August 1914, he said: 'Ten million Socialist and Labour voters in Europe, without a trace or vestige of power to stop war! ... Our demonstrations and speeches and resolutions are all alike futile. We have no means of hitting the warmongers. We simply do not count.' Hardie died on 26 September 1915. According to Fenner Brockway: 'I've never seen a man so broken, he died a year later and just as much as any soldier who was shot, he was a casualty of the war, comparatively young, not yet 60, but physically, mentally and spiritually broken by the thought that over the frontier workers were killing each other.'

A new movement

Perhaps ironically, once war started the roots of a new and unprecedented pacifist and anti-war movement began to emerge, which gathered strength as war progressed. It was as if the war itself galvanised action. The most significant element was to be the emergence of some 16,000 conscientious objectors, who came to public notice in 1916 when conscription was introduced. But even before then a number of important anti-war voices and groups were appearing, some religious, others more political in nature.

Disgusted by the Labour Party's support for the war, the ILP distanced itself, publishing a stirring manifesto in the *Labour Leader*, which stated that: 'Across the roar of guns, we send sympathy and greeting to the German Socialists ... They are no enemies of ours, but faithful friends.' Despite the pro-war climate of the time, the *Labour Leader* doubled its pre-war circulation figures to more than 40,000 by October 1914 and continued to challenge the justification for war as well as highlighting the evils of the international arms trade. It also gave space to some significant anti-war writers, including philosopher Bertrand Russell, left-wing journalist Henry Noel Brailsford and Labour MP Herbert Morrison.

There were a number of dissenting MPs within Parliament as well, mainly ILP MPs but also MPs from the Liberal and Labour parties.

They included Quaker MPs Arnold Rowntree, T.E. Harvey, J. Allen Baker and J.W. Wilson, as well as Joseph King, Arthur Ponsonby, Richard Lambert and Charles Trevelyan, who resigned his position as Secretary for Education. Other anti-war MPs included Philip Snowden, who consistently championed the rights of conscientious objectors.

Also drawn from the ranks of anti-war politicians was the Union of Democratic Control (UDC), a very significant anti-war organisation that was launched early on in the war. On 5 August 1914, Charles Trevelyan, having resigned from the Cabinet, began contacting sympathetic friends with a view to forming an anti-war organisation and together with Norman Angell and E.D. Morel, both from the Liberal Party, and Ramsay MacDonald, he launched the UDC. The UDC was effectively a coalition of members of the ILP, Labour and Liberal parties. Its main aims were to impose parliamentary control over foreign policy; to negotiate a democratic peace and ensure arbitration to avoid future conflicts, and that peace terms should neither humiliate the defeated nation, nor re-arrange frontiers, which might lead to future wars. The UDC issued a manifesto in November 1914 and by 1915 had about 100 branches, many in Scotland and the Midlands, and a membership of some 300,000 including some very influential figures. Among the more prominent members were aristocratic patron of the arts Ottoline Morrell, whose home was always open to opponents of the war, Frederick Pethick-Lawrence, husband of suffragette Emmeline Pethick-Lawrence, pacifist ILP MP Philip Snowden, author Olive Schreiner and many others. In the jingoistic climate of the time, the UDC was accused of being pro-German and elements of the popular press insisted that it was funded by Germany. Despite this the UDC continued to garner considerable support.

Not surprisingly the Society of Friends – the Quakers – remained in the forefront of the Christian peace movement. In November 1914, its executive committee, known as the 'Meeting for Sufferings', issued a Declaration on the War, which in its preamble stated that: '… all war is utterly incompatible with the plain precepts of our Divine Lord and Lawgiver, and with the whole spirit and tenor of His Gospel …'. Pacifist beliefs meant that Quakers would not pick up arms; nor were Quakers prepared to do any work that they believed would assist the war machine, although several felt they had a duty to help ameliorate the sufferings of war. A number of Quaker committees were set up to help refugees and other victims of war and many went to France to assist those made homeless by war. In September 1914 as well, a small group of Quakers organised a Quaker Ambulance Unit, later known as the Friends Ambulance Unit (FAU).

One of the first pacifist organisations to be launched was the Fellowship of Reconciliation (FoR), a Christian pacifist group. It came out of an eve of war pledge: Friedrich Siegmund-Schultze, a German Lutheran who was formerly chaplain to the German Kaiser, and Henry Hodgkin, an English Quaker, parted at Cologne station with the commitment that: 'We are one in Christ and can never be at war'. Following this event, in December 1914 Hodgkin organised a conference in Cambridge attended by more than 100 Christians of all denominations. From this emerged the Fellowship of Reconciliation. By November 1915, the FoR had 55 branches across the UK and some 1,500 members; by its end there were 165 branches and a membership of about 8,000. During the war, the FoR produced pamphlets and a regular journal, held meetings, opposed compulsory military service and provided support for conscientious objectors, working closely with the No-Conscription Fellowship (N-CF), which was formed in 1914. It fulfilled similar functions during the Second World War and remains active today. Norman Kember, the British peace activist who was kidnapped in Iraq in 2005, was one of its members.

The No-Conscription Fellowship

One organisation that would take a leading role in organising war resisters – those who would refuse to fight – was the No-Conscription Fellowship, which was first launched in November 1914. At the start of the war, entry into the army was on a voluntary basis but many people believed that conscription, or compulsory military service, would be introduced if the war were to continue – and by autumn 1914 it was clear that this war would not be over by Christmas. Given there would be men who would refuse military service on grounds of conscience, activists such as Fenner Brockway felt it would be a good idea for them to band together. Lilla Brockway, who had recently married Fenner, came up with an excellent suggestion, namely that a letter should be placed in the *Labour Leader* inviting prospective war resisters to join a N-CF. The letter duly went into the paper; the response was far greater than Brockway had anticipated:

It was my wife who suggested that those of us who would refuse military service should get together; I didn't feel I could advocate this in the columns of the *Labour Leader*, although I was editor, because in a sense it was unconstitutional action and I didn't want to commit the party [ILP] to that as a party. So I got my wife to write a letter to the paper and she did. And as a result of that names poured in of young men who would refuse to fight in the war. The interesting thing was that it was not only young socialists; it was young religious people, mostly young Quakers but others as well, Methodists, Primitive Methodists, and as all these names poured in, those who had been most active in bringing them together, formed themselves into an ad hoc committee ...

'*The response was so immediate, and the earnestness of the writers so moving, that it at once became clear that there was need for a fellowship in which the prospective resisters might unite.*'

Fenner Brockway

The new organisation attracted an initial membership of around 300 men; as the war progressed this increased to about 12,000. One of the earliest members was Clifford Allen, later Lord Allen of Hurtwood, who was then aged 25. Born in South Wales to an Anglican and conservative family, Allen won a scholarship to Cambridge, where he became a socialist and pacifist. After university he joined the Labour Party's newspaper, the *Daily Citizen*. In 1914 he wrote a pamphlet 'Is Germany Right and England Wrong?' in which he argued against Britain's involvement in the war. A tall, slight and frail man, he was an inspirational speaker and greatly admired. When the first committee was formed, Allen became chairman of the N-CF with Fenner Brockway as secretary. Also on the committee was Clarence Henry (C.H.) Norman, a political activist and member of the ILP. According to Brockway, Norman was a 'startling and provocative individualist, with ideas and proposals which took away our breath'.

The N-CF was without doubt an extraordinary organisation and some have described it as the most significant peace organisation in Britain; one conscientious objector remarked that it was the 'most abused institution in England'. And it certainly did come in for a lot of

The Women's Peace Congress, 1915: a bold initiative

On 28 April 1915, as war raged in Europe, more than 1,200 women from 12 different countries, including Britain, Germany, Austria-Hungary, Italy, Poland, Belgium and the United States met at The Hague, in the Netherlands, and convened what became known as the Women's Peace Congress. Many of the women were feminists, who had been active in fighting for the vote. Among them was American feminist and pacifist Jane Addams, who ran Hull House in Chicago, a settlement for poor immigrants. Also there was Hungarian Rosika Schwimmer, founder of the Hungarian Association of Working Women. Three British women attended: Emmeline Pethick-Lawrence, a suffragette and one of the early founders of the Women's Social and Political Union, pacifist and welfare worker Emily Hobhouse, who exposed the horror of British concentration camps in South Africa during the Boer War and whose cousin Stephen Hobhouse would become a well-known conscientious objector, and Chrystal Macmillan, pacifist and women's rights activist.

Getting to the peace congress had not been easy; not only was it dangerous to attempt to travel during wartime but also the women were constantly ridiculed. Former President Theodore described the American delegates as 'both silly and base', while the popular press delighted in ridiculing the women as 'peacettes'. In Britain, where war had completely split the women's movement, 150 women applied for passports to attend the Congress but only 25 women were granted them and when they reached Tilbury docks they found that the North Sea had been closed to shipping. The three British women who finally reached The Hague only got there because they came from outside Britain. The popular press had a field day belittling their efforts.

The Congress was the result of an invitation from a Dutch women's suffrage organisation, headed by Aletta Jacobs, to women's rights organisations worldwide to meet and discuss ways in which women might be able to bring the war to an end. In her opening address on 28 April, Aletta Jacobs set the tone of the Congress, saying:

We grieve for the many brave young men who have lost their lives on the battlefield ... we mourn with the poor mothers bereft of their sons, with the thousands of young widows and fatherless children, and we feel that we can no longer endure in the twentieth century of civilization that governments should tolerate brute force as the only solution of international disputes.

Over the following three days the women debated what should be their best course of action, deciding in favour of a non-violent form of conflict resolution and for continuous mediation to be implemented, without armistice, until peace could be restored. The Congress issued a set of resolutions and also founded the Women's International League for Peace and Freedom, which is still active today.

What was also decided was to send delegates from the Congress to governments of the warring countries in an attempt to mediate for peace. Following the Congress, between May and June delegates visited fourteen capital cities, including Washington, meeting with individual leaders. Initially, women were received fairly sympathetically but as the war intensified and casualties mounted, including the sinking of the *Lusitania* in May, with more than 1,000 dead, including 38 babies and 100 Americans, any support for the women's cause died away. Delegates returned to their own countries and although they had not succeeded in ending the war, most remained active in the anti-war movement, supporting conscientious objectors in their own countries.

abuse. Even so, despite press and public vilification, police surveillance and raids, and the fact that nearly all its organisers and most members went to prison, the N-CF continued its work as the leading organisation for conscientious objectors until it was disbanded in 1919. From 1916 it produced a weekly newspaper, the *Tribunal*, which never failed to appear even though the offices were frequently raided. It worked ceaselessly not just for conscientious objectors but also for their families and dependents. It provided advice and support for COs already in prison or waiting to be imprisoned; recorded all events relating to COs; produced articles and pamphlets and generally established a remarkable network of information and support, attending tribunals, lobbying Parliament and keeping conscientious objectors constantly informed about events. Taken altogether, the N-CF provided not just a hub for COs but also inspiration and leadership, effectively bringing conscientious objectors together in what has been described as the CO movement.

This is not to say that the N-CF was always united: commenting on the diversity and individualism of members, Howard Marten, a Quaker and conscientious objector, remembered that:

> the ranks of the No-Conscription Fellowship were made up of men from every conceivable walk of life. You had all sorts of religious groups from the Salvation Army to the Seventh Day Adventists, Church of England, Roman Catholics; there was no limit. It was a sort of cross-section of every time ... in addition ... the more politically minded: the Independent Labour Party, and different degrees of socialists ... Then a very curious group of what I used to call artistically minded ... the aesthetic group: artists, musicians, all that ...

According to Fenner Brockway:

> Although the N-CF was based on the principle of the "sacredness of human life" its membership extended beyond absolute pacifists. In its branches, scattered throughout the country, were Socialists, Anarchists, Quakers, and other religious objectors, and it was remarkable how well they pulled together. From the first, however, the movement was much more than an expression of personal objection to military service, it was political.

Despite differences in views, however, what the N-CF helped to do was to create a sense of comradeship and support for men who were going to take a very drastic step that would put them outside the law: namely to resist conscription and call-up but in November 1914 that step was still some way off. In the N-CF's early stages the Brockways' cottage in Derbyshire provided an informal headquarters for the new organisation, with Lilla Brockway acting as informal secretary. The committee held what Brockway described as a 'watching brief,' ready to act should an emergency arise. That emergency would be conscription but in late 1914 and early 1915, committee members were constantly assured that conscription would not be introduced. Nevertheless, membership grew steadily; local groups were set up throughout the country and by early 1915, the membership had increased so considerably that the N-CF opened an office in London. From this point the N-CF's work intensified as it became increasingly likely that conscription would be introduced in Britain and that men who wanted to resist military service on grounds of conscience would need a solid organisation behind them.

Chapter 2

Conscription and Conscience

'We, the members of the No-Conscription Fellowship … hereby solemnly and sincerely affirm our intention to resist conscription, whatever the penalties may be.'

When war began so-called 'war fever' swept through the nation. Xenophobia was the order of the day as rumours about German spies and the 'enemy within' filled the pages of the popular press. Thousands of young men, some underage, flocked to join the army, desperate to get into the fray before it all ended. The shift in public attitude from an unwillingness to be involved in a European war to a mood that was nationalistic and militaristic was dramatic. Writing in the *Nation* on 15 August 1914, Bertrand Russell, who was to become actively involved with the N-CF, described the change as he saw it:

A month ago Europe was a peaceful group of nations: if an Englishman killed a German, he was hanged. Now, if an Englishman kills a German, or if a German kills an Englishman, he is a patriot. We scan the newspapers with greedy eyes for news of slaughter, and rejoice when we read of innocent young men, blindly obedient to the word of command, mown down in thousands by the machine-gun of Liege. Those who saw the London crowds, during the nights leading up to the Declaration of War saw a whole population, hitherto peaceable and humane, precipitated in a few days down the steep slope to primitive barbarism, letting loose, in a moment, the instincts of hatred and blood lust against which the whole fabric of society has been raised.

Eager recruits

In 1914 Britain was the only one of the Great Powers that did not have conscription, or compulsory military service. Entry into the army was on a voluntary basis and this did not change when war began. Nor at first did it have to: urged on by propaganda, excitement, a wish to join up with one's peers, and in some cases the desire to get out of desperately poor conditions, young men flocked to the army. The newspapers were full of alleged atrocities in Belgium and most men even if they had some doubts felt it was their duty to go to war. Lord Kitchener, hero of the Sudan and Boer War and newly appointed Secretary of State for War, told men that 'Your Country Needs You' and they responded. For Private F.B. Vaughan, who served with the 12th battalion, Yorks and Lancs:

> my pals were going, chaps I had kicked about with in the street … when you went to the pictures you'd be shown crowds of young men drilling in Hyde Park or crowding round the recruiting office, or it might be a band playing 'Tipperary'. The whole thing was exciting … We were stirred … by the atrocities, or the alleged atrocities, when the Germans invaded Belgium and France.

Women too were used to encourage recruitment. Images of women and children appeared on recruiting posters, urging their men to defend Britain, while some women handed out white feathers – traditional symbol of cowardice – to men not in uniform. The White Feather Organisation, which was the brainchild of Admiral Charles Fitzgerald, emerged in August 1914 and was eagerly supported by, among others, writer Mrs Humphrey Ward, who was strongly opposed to votes for women, and militant suffragette turned patriotic government supporter Mrs Emmeline Pankhurst. The campaign reflected the public mood at the time and certainly forced some men to enlist rather than be humiliated. By contrast Fenner Brockway, certain of his stand, proudly claimed he had received enough white feathers to make a fan.

During the first three months of the war recruits flooded in at a rate of 300,000 men a month. By the end of September 1914, more than 750,000 men had enlisted; by January 1915, the number had reached 1 million. Strictly speaking, only men aged between 18 and 38 were eligible, but there were many instances of underage men joining up as well as those who were older. Young recruits were not supposed to be sent abroad until they were 19 but again men younger than that were in the trenches.

At first the response was so overwhelming that the War Office struggled to equip, house and prepare recruits for combat. However, as the early months gave way to stalemate in the trenches of the Western Front and as the death and injury toll mounted – 12,733 casualties at the first Battle of the Marne in October 1914 and 55,395 casualties at the first Battle of Ypres, October–November 1914 – by January 1915 the numbers of voluntary recruits had dropped to 120,000 men a month; by April 1915 the figure was about 80,000 men a month. As it became increasingly clear that this would be a long, bitter war of attrition – something Kitchener had foreseen – it became equally apparent that more men would be needed and the issue of conscription became a major talking point.

The road to conscription
Even before the war various individuals and groups had been calling for conscription or compulsory military training. In 1902 the National Service League was formed, under the presidency of Lord Raglan and subsequently Field Marshal Lord Roberts. It had lobbied hard for conscription, arguing that the British army was inadequate and that implementing compulsory national service along European lines would produce a more efficient force. Newspaper magnate Lord Northcliffe promoted the idea of compulsion through his newspapers, particularly the very popular *Daily Mail*. Support grew, attracting a number of influential people, among them writer Rudyard Kipling and most Conservative members of Parliament.

Despite this there was not much public support for conscription before 1914. There was a general feeling that forcing men into the forces smacked of the old press-gangs and that anyway forcibly enlisted men did not make the best soldiers. Conscription was not seen as suiting the British way of life: in the words of the H.J. Tennant, Parliamentary Under Secretary of State for War, during a debate in the House of Commons in May 1915, it was 'foreign to the British nation, to the British character, and to the genius of our people', though Tennant admitted that in certain circumstances it might become necessary. A number of bills proposing some sort of compulsory military training were introduced into Parliament but were either withdrawn or defeated. In March 1913, Mr Sandys MP introduced a

National Services (Territorial) Bill in the House of Commons, arguing that with the build up of forces in Germany, Britain needed to introduce compulsion. Keir Hardie and others opposed it and it did not go to a vote. A year later, in March 1914, Prime Minister Asquith turned down a deputation from the National Service League.

When war began the Cabinet was divided on the question of conscription: most Conservative MPs supported it, while the majority of Liberals did not. Labour MPs including members of the ILP were strongly opposed. In August 1914 Lord Kitchener stated that voluntary recruitment would be sufficient but also stated that, 'if the war should be protracted ... exertions and sacrifices beyond any which have been demanded will be required from the whole nation and the Empire, and where they are required we are sure they will not be denied in the extreme needs of the State by Parliament or the people.' Prime Minister Asquith said there were no plans for conscription at that time but on 8 January 1915 during a debate in the House of Lords, Haldane, the Lord Chancellor, said that, while he thought compulsion would be a 'bad thing', in a time of national emergency 'any other consideration must yield to national interest.' On 20 April Mr Thomas Tickler MP for Grimsby asked the Prime Minister if he would introduce conscription for the purposes of 'prosecuting the War with all the available forces of the Empire. ... And thereby saving the lives of thousands of our soldiers by bringing the War to a speedy and successful termination.' Answering on behalf of Asquith, Lloyd George, who would soon be appointed Minister for Munitions, replied that the government was 'not of the opinion that there is any ground for thinking that the War would be more successfully prosecuted by means of conscription' and that the government was satisfied with the rate of recruitment. Not long after, Lloyd George shifted ground in support of conscription.

Although by now the public mood was increasingly keen on conscription, not least married women who were angered that their husbands were in the trenches while single men were still refusing to volunteer, the government still balked at all-out conscription and in June 1915 introduced a National Registration Bill. It was described by Walter Long, President of the Local Government Boards, as a 'grand voluntary movement to secure knowledge of the forces which the country possesses' but very few believed this. For anti-conscriptionists, such as the members of the N-CF, the National Registration Bill was the first step towards compulsion.

Despite opposition by pacifist MPs such as Philip Snowden, who argued that the Bill was a forerunner of compulsory military service, stating in the House of Commons on 5 July 1915 that 'the idea of compulsion has run through every speech in support of the Bill this afternoon ...', the Bill passed its final reading by 259 votes to 16 and became law on 8 July 1915. Under the Act all British civilians – men and women – aged 15–65 had to fill in a form stating their name, age, marital status, employment details and whether they were prepared to volunteer for any special form of work. Philip Snowden suggested that the upper age limit should be raised to 75 on the grounds that 'This war is really an old man's war in the sense that it is the old men who are responsible ...', but needless to say, his suggestion was shouted down.

Registration was compulsory; those who did not register could be fined. On registering – registration day was 15 August – each person received a certificate. By September 1915 it was discovered from the register's figures that some 5 million men of military age were not serving in the forces. Excluding those in 'starred' or essential work, and those unfit to serve, it was estimated that somewhere in the region of 1,700,000–1,800,000 eligible men had not volunteered.

Efforts to get these men into the army intensified. Music hall stars such as Vesta Tilley, who gained a reputation as 'England's Greatest Recruiting Sergeant', Marie Lloyd and Harry Lauder toured the country, appealing to patriotism and duty, urging men to join up. Posters asking 'Daddy, What did YOU do in the Great War?' attempted to shame men to take the enlistment plunge and the white-feather campaign continued apace. Speaking from the pulpits, ministers in many churches also exhorted their male flocks to rally to the needs of the nation, something that seriously shocked many religious conscientious objectors. Recruitment committees urged men to sign up, sometimes backing up the suggestion with implicit threats that if men did not sign up, they would be fetched.

Registration was followed by what was known as the 'Derby Scheme', named after Lord Derby who had been appointed Director of Recruiting. Under this scheme, and working from the registration records, recruiting officers personally canvassed every eligible man aged 18–41, pressing them to 'attest' or commit to join the army when needed. Those who did so took a military oath and were given an armband; they were also assured that attested men would be called up by age, single men being called before married men. Exemptions were possible for employed men whose employers considered they were indispensable and tribunals were set up to hear applications for exemption.

By now very few people believed that voluntary recruitment was going to produce the numbers of men that the army needed and in fact the Derby Scheme, which ran until the end of November, only produced a further 340,000 recruits out of a potential 2,200,000.

The Military Service Act, 1916

By December 1915 British casualties had reached 528,227, at least one-third of whom were dead or missing. On 21 December Asquith asked Parliament's authorisation to call up another million men and by 28 December Cabinet had agreed the terms of a Military Service Bill, which would impose conscription from March 1916 for all single men aged 18–41, with some exceptions. Asquith introduced the Bill to the House of Commons on 5 January 1916, stating that it was one 'which can be sincerely supported by those who, either on principle, or, as my own case, on grounds of expediency, are opposed to what is commonly described as conscription.' There was opposition, led by Sir John Smith who claimed there was no support for the Bill in the country but the Bill went through its second reading and on 17 January went to the House of Commons for each clause to be ratified and/or amended and on 27 January 1916 it became law. Conscription had arrived in Britain.

Under the terms of the Military Service Act, every unmarried or widowed man, who had no dependents, aged 19–41 was 'deemed to have enlisted for general service with the colours or in the reserve', that is they all effectively became soldiers as of 2 March 1916, which is when the Act came into effect. The date itself prompted a poster campaign that asked 'Will you march too or wait until March 2?' in an effort to bring in men before the start date. There were exceptions: the Act did not apply to men already in the army or reserves, or who had been discharged from the army because of ill health; men who were normally resident abroad but were only in Britain to study or some other 'special' purpose; men serving in the navy or Royal Marines; priests or other religious ministers; and men who already had a certificate of exemption.

The Act also included four grounds on which men could apply for exemption from military service. These were: if a man was employed in work of national importance; ill health or infirmity; if serious hardship would be caused to a dependent; and if he had a 'conscientious objection to the undertaking of combatant service'. Any exemption could be absolute, conditional or temporary. In April conscription was extended to married men.

The conscience clause

Given the patriotic and militaristic mood of the time, mounting casualties and the demand for more soldiers, it seems rather extraordinary that the Military Service Act should have included provision for conscientious objectors. And when the Bill was first drafted in December 1915, there was no such provision: there were only three grounds on which men could apply for exemption from military service – conscientious objection was not one of them.

However, when the final draft of the Bill was put in front of the House of Commons in January 1916, a conscience clause had been added. Exactly why this happened is not absolutely clear. Certainly the activities of N-CF as well as the known views of Quakers and other religious groups opposed to engaging in combat meant that Asquith and others knew there would be men who would refuse military service on grounds of conscience. Christadelphians had petitioned Parliament in February 1915 for legal exemption and the N-CF, though opposed to conscription but recognising that it would probably be introduced, lobbied for a conscience clause based on precedence established for conscientious objection to compulsory smallpox vaccination. Under an act of 1898 a statutory declaration of conscientious objection sworn before a magistrate was sufficient.

Whether lobbying by the N-CF and others influenced the final decision is difficult to assess. It is probably more likely that Asquith, aware of Liberal, Quaker and ILP opposition to the Bill, felt it would be politically expedient to make provision. Either way, when the final draft was put before Cabinet on 1 January it included a conscience clause allowing men to apply for exemption who had 'a conscientious objection to undertaking combatant service'.

Asquith presented the Military Service Bill to a packed House of Commons on 5 January 1915, many MPs being dressed in full military uniform. Describing the Bill as one that 'can be sincerely supported by those who, either on principle, or, as in my own case, on grounds of expediency, are opposed to what is commonly described as conscription', he went on to outline its terms. When he came to the provision for conscientious objectors there was, according to the *Daily Mail*, an 'outburst of incredulous and contemptuous cries ... The laughter was long and loud'. Expressing his sorrow at this reaction, Asquith stated that there were precedents for this clause, namely that Quakers had been exempted from combat during the French Wars and that more recently Quakers were exempted from military service in Australia and South Africa. He went on to say: 'there are a great many people belonging to various religious denominations, or to various schools of thought, who are quite prepared to serve their country in the War, but who object, on conscientious grounds, to the taking of life. They are, however, quite willing to perform many other duties ...' As it turned out, Asquith's belief that COs would perform 'many other duties' showed he had very little understanding of the complexity of conscientious objection, not least that objectors would not only resist being conscripted into combat and killing but also being conscripted into anything that might be seen as assisting the war effort or enabling others to kill.

The conscience clause was discussed as the Bill went through its various readings. Some opponents wanted it taken out completely. Others wanted changes. Mr Joynson-Hicks, MP for Brentford wanted conscientious objection to apply only to Quakers and other religious objectors; Major Newman suggested the clause should be amended to apply to 'the taking of human life' rather than combatant service, while Quaker MP Edmund Harvey proposed the clause be widened to cover 'conscientious objection to the undertaking of military service or combatant service'. During a debate in the House of Lords, Lord Courtney of Penwith proposed that the clause should read, 'conscientious objection to undertake any service or engage in any activity in support of the war or to the undertaking of combatant service ...', which demonstrated a much clearer understanding of the CO's position. In the event the original wording stayed so that the conscience clause referred only to 'combatant service', something that was to cause considerable problems. It was decided also that those claiming conscientious objection would appear before tribunals, which would rule on the outcomes.

Opposing conscription
From 1913 the ILP and other sections of the labour movement had vociferously opposed conscription. In *A Case Against Conscription*

(1913), Keir Hardie had written: 'Compulsory military service is the negation of democracy. It compels the youth of the country, under penalty of a fine and imprisonment, to learn the art of war. That is despotism, not democracy. No liberty-loving people will tolerate having these old forms of servitude forced upon them. Conscription is the badge of the slave.'

While the ILP protested against conscription for largely pacifist and civil liberty reasons, the mainstream Labour Party and the labour movement also opposed conscription, not so much on pacifist grounds but more from a fear that with military conscription would come industrial compulsion, forcing workers into work on terms dictated by the government. In September 1915 the Trades Union Congress overwhelmingly passed a resolution stating their opposition to conscription. That month too Asquith, replying to a parliamentary question, stated that he had received some 400 resolutions from labour organisations, all of them opposing conscription.

In October 1915, by which time the Derby Scheme was in operation, the ILP held Stop Conscription meetings across the country, addressed by pacifists such as George Lansbury, who would later be leader of the Labour Party, and suffragette Sylvia Pankhurst, who had decisively broken away from her pro-war mother and sister.

However, in the last stages of the debate on the Military Service Bill, the Labour revolt collapsed. A government commitment that industrial conscription would not be introduced, combined with the fact that the Derby Scheme, which could be seen as the dying gasp of volunteerism, had manifestly failed to produce the numbers required, meant that their opposition faded away. The ILP maintained its anti-conscription stand but as a group was becoming increasingly isolated.

Preparing to resist

The N-CF spearheaded opposition to conscription, not surprising given its name. Initially, the N-CF had held what Fenner Brockway described as a 'watching brief' but from July 1915, when the danger of conscription became imminent, the organisation swung into action. It organised a 'lightning campaign', setting up branches throughout the country and exploring strategies for men who would resist conscription should it be introduced. Together with the FoR and the Friends' Service Committees, the N-CF set up a Joint Advisory Council to co-ordinate activities as and when appropriate.

In August compulsory registration was introduced. The N-CF advised potential resisters or conscientious objectors to register but to state in writing that on grounds of conscience they would not take part in military service, war related work or in the manufacture of armaments or other products related to taking the human life.

In September 1915, the N-CF issued a manifesto publicly stating its position very clearly and its grounds for resisting conscription:

> The case for and against compulsory military and munition service is being argued by many who, for reasons of age or sex, would not be subject to it. The signatories of this Manifesto think it imperative to voice a protest in the name of a large body of men in this country who, though able-bodied and of military age, will – in the event of coercive measures – be bound by deep conscientious conviction to decline these services, whatever the consequences of refusal.
>
> We yield to no one in our admiration of the self-sacrifice, the courage and the unflagging devotion of those of our fellow-countrymen who have felt it their duty to take up arms. Nevertheless, we cannot undertake the same form of service; our conviction is solemn and unalterable.
>
> Whatever the purpose to be achieved by war, however high the ideals for which belligerent nations may struggle, for us 'Thou shalt not kill' means what it says. The destruction of our fellow-men – young men like ourselves – appals us; we cannot assist in the cutting off of one generation from life's opportunities. Insistence upon individual obligations in the interests of national well-being has no terrors for us; we gladly admit – we would even extend – the right of the community to impose duties upon its members for the common good, but we deny the right of any Government to make the slaughter of our fellows a bounden duty ...

The manifesto went on to say that although members had different reasons for arriving at this stand, all believed 'in the value and sacredness of human personality, and are prepared to sacrifice as much in the cause of the world's peace as our fellows are sacrificing in the cause of the nation's war ...'.

The signatories to the manifesto were Clifford Allen, Fenner Brockway and N-CF treasurer Edward Grubb. Around 20,000 copies of the manifesto were distributed which well and truly brought the N-CF to the attention of the government and authorities. A number of N-CF members were prosecuted and fined for publishing and distributing anti-conscription leaflets and the N-CF offices began to come under police surveillance.

Launching the resistance

Realising that 'the testing time', namely conscription, was approaching, the N-CF made detailed plans to safeguard the organisation, which had already been described as 'seditious' in the House of Commons, a decision that proved particularly effective when its leaders were taken off to prison. Each N-CF official at national and local level had a 'shadow' or duplicate who could take over if someone was arrested. Communication networks were set up so that information could be passed secretly and misinformation was frequently issued to put the authorities off the scent. The organisation also created different sections to deal with different aspects of their work. These included a records department that kept detailed information on each CO from appearances at tribunals through to prison; a visitation department that maintained contact with and organised visits to COs in guardrooms and prisons across the country; a press department; a campaign department; a literature section that produced leaflets and pamphlets; and a press department.

In November 1915 the N-CF held its first national convention in London. By now the Derby Scheme was all but finished and it was clear that conscription was the next step. In its 'statement of faith', the Fellowship described itself an organisation of:

> men likely to be called upon to undertake military service in the event of conscription, who will refuse from conscientious motives to bear arms, because they consider human life to be sacred, and cannot, therefore, assume the responsibility of inflicting death. They deny the right of the Government to say, 'You shall bear arms', and will oppose every effort to introduce compulsory military service into Great Britain. Should such efforts be successful, they will, whatever the consequences may be, obey their conscientious convictions rather than the commands of Governments.

Clifford Allen made a long and stirring speech saying that the N-CF was not just a propaganda machine but would actively resist conscription should conscription arrive. He said that although members might differ on their reasons for conscientiously refusing conscription, one thing united them all, namely the 'sanctity of human life'. He argued that the State had no right to tell a man to take up arms to kill another man in times of war, such a decision was up to individual conscience alone and that the Fellowship would oppose all attempts by the State to force this decision. He finished his speech by asking members to stand in silence and consider a resolution that affirmed their position:

> That we, the delegates and members of the No-Conscription Fellowship, assembled in National Conference, fully conscious of the attempt that may be made to impose conscription on this country, recognising that such a system must destroy the sanctity of human life, betray the free traditions of our country and hinder its social and industrial emancipation, though realizing the grave consequences to ourselves that may follow our decision, hereby solemnly and sincerely reaffirm our intention to resist conscription, whatever the penalties may be.

The resolution was adopted: whether the organisers realised it at the time or not, a powerful resistance movement had been launched that would profoundly challenge the authority of the State.

Writing in his autobiographical *Inside the Left*, Brockway described how the N-CF's first national convention was met by a storm of abuse from the press: 'I suppose the editors thought they would kill us with contempt by printing ghastly pictures of the "platform", with captions referring to us as "cowards", "Hun-lovers", "The save-their-skins-brigade", and "The won't-fight funks", but the effect was exactly the opposite. Applications for membership overwhelmed us.'

Another who experienced anger from the public was Harold Bing. He and his father joined the Croydon branch of the N-CF. His sister Dorothy, who was too young at that point, joined later. In an interview with the Imperial War Museum (IWM), Bing described the reaction of the general public to the resisters:

> My father saw a notice about it [N-CF] in one of the newspapers …
> and we became active in it. I became literature secretary for the few
> months that I was still at liberty … By this time those who were

going to oppose conscription were coming together, meeting one another and making plans and the anti-conscription movement was beginning to formulate itself … a number of meetings were held, they were often broken up and speakers were thrown into ponds and otherwise maltreated. I was on one occasion distributing literature house to house, anti-war literature house to house and was pursued by an infuriated householder who saw the literature, quickly came out and chased me for a long distance until he lost me in the darkness carrying with him a very heavy stick.

As Clifford Allen and others had already indicated, resisting conscription was not going to be easy. Harry Stanton was a Quaker and pacifist. When he turned 21 he set up the Luton branch of the N-CF. He knew resistance would be easier working with others:

As conscription became more and more inevitable, those of us who had adopted the pacifist attitude began to consider wither our opposition would lead us. For an individual to attempt to resist the power of the state would be a tremendous venture. The number of persons prepared to make such an attempt must be very small but they would be infinitely stronger if they could form a common plan of action.

When the Military Service Bill was first introduced into Parliament, the N-CF produced and distributed more than a million leaflets, held hundreds of meetings and sent deputations to the House of Commons. Despite intensive lobbying, the Bill passed its third reading and became law on 28 January 1916. The Act would be implemented on 2 March 1916 on which date the first batch of men would be called up. The plan was to call up men by age groups; initially single men but from April, married men as well. Those who refused their call-up would face at the very least fines and probably imprisonment, although at that stage no one was absolutely certain what would happen. With conscription now in place, N-CF members and others outside the Fellowship readied themselves to resist conscription and take their stand as conscientious objectors. As such they would be breaking the law but were prepared to take the consequences.

A tumultuous convention
In April 1916, as the first COs were being arrested for refusing to accept call-up papers, the N-CF held a second national convention at Devonshire House, then the headquarters of the Society of Friends in London. Some 2,000 men, from 198 branches around the country, packed the building. The convention lasted for two days and was very dramatic both inside and outside the building. The popular press was doing its best to whip up public anger against conscientious objectors, who in the eyes of most of the public were shirkers, cowards and even traitors for refusing to fight. An angry crowd had assembled outside the building and as Fenner Brockway arrived he was handed a copy of *John Bull*, a sensationalist pro-war magazine published by Horatio Bottomley, former MP and financial swindler. With a front-page cover headed 'Take Him to the Tower', the magazine included an article demanding the arrest and execution of Brockway. Ironically, when Brockway was first arrested, he was taken to the Tower of London – but not executed.

Probably organised by the press, a group of sailors attempted to attack the building; the iron gates were locked but two or three sailors managed to climb over and get into the convention, where the reception they received was not what they had expected. According to Brockway's account: 'Inside, instead of fists, friendly hands were extended to them. They stood perplexed, cut off from their supporters, surrounded by the hated "Pro-Germans", yet finding them the best of fellows. The sailors stayed to take tea with the stewards, and left with a very different idea about "conchies".'

The convention continued with its business, which was essentially to establish a framework for resistance to conscription and military service. As speeches and debates took place, hecklers outside jeered, hurled insults and continued threatening to break into the building, their anger increasing when they heard clapping from inside. Clifford Allan, who was chairing the convention, suggested that in order not to enrage the crowds outside any further, delegates should adopt a strategy of silent support for speakers, showing their enthusiasm by waving handkerchiefs or papers rather than by clapping. As Brockway described: 'No one who was present will readily forget the effect of this. When Philip Snowden, Dr John Clifford and Bertrand Russell rose to speak they were received with thousands of fluttering handkerchiefs, making the low sound of rising and falling wind, but with no other sound whatsoever.'

Despite the anger of the crowds, the convention continued to the great enthusiasm of all delegates. Clifford Allen made a moving and impassioned address, spelling out clearly to the government that members of the Fellowship, nearly all of whom were young men of military age, would resist conscription and were 'willing to undergo the penalties that the State may inflict – yes, even death itself – rather than go back upon our convictions'. Having come to the end of his speech, he moved the following resolution, which mirrored the original manifesto. Standing in silence, the delegates adopted it, so laying the basis for an extraordinary network that united conscientious objectors throughout the country.

> That we, representing thousands of men who cannot participate in warfare, and yet are subject to the terms of the Military Service Act, unite in comradeship with those of our number who are already suffering for conscience' sake in prison or in the hands of the military. We appreciate the spirit of sacrifice which actuates those who are suffering on the battlefield and in the same spirit we renew our determination, whatever the penalties awaiting us, to undertake no service which for us is wrong. We are confident that thus we shall advance the cause of peace and so render such service to our fellow-men in all nations as will contribute to the healing of the wounds inflicted by war.

The 'conchies'

Based on N-CF membership alone, it was clear that several hundred, if not thousands of men, would be prepared to break the law by resisting conscription and military service on grounds of conscience. In the event about 16,000 men took their stand as conscientious objectors and a new word 'conchies' entered the English language, a term used by much of the popular press to insult and denigrate them. However, just as militant activists in the fight for the vote seized on the word 'suffragette', first used as an insult by the *Daily Mail* in 1909, so too many COs chose to describe themselves as 'conchies'.

So who were they, the men who took this remarkable stand at a time when virtually the whole country believed it was a man's duty to fight for King and country? By definition, all of them were of military age and many of them were still in their twenties. They included a wide variety of men from different social and political backgrounds, whose reasons for taking such a daring and unpopular stand varied, from religious through to moral, humanitarian and political beliefs. As well as the more prominent members of the N-CF such as Clifford Allen, Fenner Brockway, Walter Ayles, A. Barratt Brown and Aylmer Rose, conscientious objectors included men such as Henry Sargent, a keen naturalist and skilled artist who went on to become the highly respected curator of Bexhill Museum after the war. Very few local residents knew that their respectable curator had broken rocks in Dartmoor during the First World War. Others included Stephen Hobhouse, son of a highly privileged and well-connected family who rejected his privilege to join the Society of Friends and live and work with the poor in the East End of London; Hubert Peet, journalist and organising secretary of the Friends' Service Committee; Richard Porteous, a young student and son of a Presbyterian minister; and Corder Catchpool, a Quaker who was working as an engineer when war began. Both Catchpool and Porteous worked in France with the FAU. Another conscientious objector was David Thomas, whose son and granddaughter I met when researching this book. David Thomas was from a working class background and according to his granddaughter, Angharad Tomos, could not afford higher education. He left school aged 14 and became a pupil teacher, eventually finding work as a primary school teacher in Talysarn, North Wales. He was according to his family a staunch socialist and pioneered the ILP and the Labour Party in North Wales, acting as agent for the first Labour MP in Caernarfon. Strongly anti-war, he wrote to the local press when conscription was introduced, comparing it with enforced prostitution.

Conscientious objectors included men from very privileged backgrounds and others from more humble origins. They were clerks, engineers, journalists, post-office workers, teachers and lecturers, watchmakers, chemists, skilled artisans, parliamentary candidates and local councillors. They included lawyers, such as Scott Duckers who wrote a book about his experiences, builders, intellectuals, thinkers, artists, musicians and farmers.

There were religious and political objectors and some who were both. They included socialists, Marxists, anarchists and Liberals. Not surprisingly many COs were Quakers but there were also Methodists, Anglicans, Christadelphians, Plymouth Brethren and Jehovah's Witnesses.

Many COs based their objection on what they considered to be the fundamental message of Christianity, namely 'thou shalt not kill'. The doctor and pacifist Dr Alfred Salter, who after the war became Labour MP for Bermondsey, made possibly one of the most powerful and dramatic statements expressing the Christian stand. Soon after the outbreak of war, Salter wrote 'The Religion of a C.O.', which was published in the *Labour Leader* on 24 September 1914. About 1½ million copies were distributed in Britain and it was translated into many other languages:

> In the matter of this war I must try to picture to myself Christ as an Englishman, with England at war with Germany ... Look! Christ in khaki, out in France, thrusting His bayonet into the body of a German workman. See! The Son of God with a machine-gun, ambushing a column of German infantry, catching them unawares in a lane and mowing them down in their helplessness. Hark! The Man of Sorrows in a cavalry charge, cutting, hacking, thrusting, crushing, cheering. No! That picture is an impossible one, *and we all know it*. That settles the matter for me. I cannot uphold the war.

Another CO, Howard Marten, also took religion as the basis for his stand: 'Even as far back as the Boer War, I felt that war was inconsistent with our Christian beliefs. I was at school at the time and enjoyed a certain amount of unpopularity because of my pacifist views, and there was a good deal of violence towards what they called the "pro Boers" – the epithet which was flung at pacifists.'

John (also known as Bert) Brocklesby came from a Wesleyan Methodist family but later became a Quaker. For him killing was incompatible with his religious beliefs. In his unpublished memoirs, 'Escape from Paganism', which are housed in the Quaker Library, in London, Brocklesby describes how:

> As a small child it was deeply impressed on me how easily one may kill another person or perhaps cause permanent injury ... merely by careless, thoughtless, foolish or uncontrolled behaviour ... I had ... no enmity nor hatred for any person. Still less could I have hatred for any German. Not only was I unable but it seemed immoral at the behest of the government to start killing millions of people I had never seen ...

Brocklesby was on a cycling holiday when the war broke out: '...we saw a placard announcing "Britain declares war on Germany" ... The first signs of war madness soon appeared ... the papers reported thousands of recruits volunteering for service. Here I may record my first conviction. However many might volunteer yet would I not ... in my mind God had called me to work for his kingdom ... God had not put me on the earth to go destroying his own children.' His pacifism did not go down too well with the people in his local community. A lay preacher, in January 1915 he was appointed to conduct the evening service in his local chapel and affirmed that the war was against the teachings of Jesus: 'What a bombshell I had unwittingly dropped'. There was enormous criticism of his sermon; a week later he preached at the Swinton Wesleyan Methodist church. Brocklesby was not the only CO to be shocked that leading Church personnel became ardent recruiters for 'what I could only regard as the Devil's work. I was horrified that the pulpits of Methodists churches should become recruiting platforms.'

A conundrum
Brocklesby gained his 'first lesson in international pacifism' from a young German, August Walter, who had left Germany to avoid conscription and was known locally as a pacifist. One day, aged about 11, Brocklesby saw August and called out 'Pro-Boer'. He then dodged out of sight.

August came upstairs and asked me if the Methodists were praying for victory. I said they were. He then told me that Paul Krueger was a Christian. Did I suppose he was praying for victory? I supposed so. 'Well,' he remarked, 'that puts God into a fix, doesn't it?' ... I remembered that when fourteen years later we were again praying for victory.

Religion was not the only driving force. Many COs were socialists and it was their political views and belief in the brotherhood of man that caused them to resist conscription and take an anti-war stand. Clifford Allen described himself as a socialist, as was Fenner Brockway, who in his tribunal statement said: 'I am a Socialist and my Socialism is based on a belief in the sacredness of human life and the unity of all human lives ... War is the antithesis of Socialism. It destroys human life and denies the unity of humanity. To participate in war would be to outrage my conscientious and most deeply held convictions. I cannot do it.'

Absolutists or alternativists

What all COs had in common was their refusal to accept conscription and to pick up arms. Beyond this point, however, there were further differences about what was the 'correct' stand to take, something that was hotly debated within the N-CF, whose committee was sometimes known as the 'Committee of Sixes and Sevens' because there was often so much disagreement.

Broadly speaking conscientious objectors fell into two main categories: those who were 'absolutists' and were not prepared to co-operate with the State and the war machine in any way. As well as refusing combatant service, they resisted direction into non-combatant service and were not prepared to be directed into alternative service, something that those who framed the Military Service Act had not anticipated. Most absolutists served very long prison sentences.

The second group were known as 'alternativists', in that they would not accept conscription into the military, nor would they pick up a weapon, but they were prepared to do some sort of 'alternative service', provided it did not run counter to their deeply held principles and contribute to the furtherance of the war.

The issue of which position conscientious objectors should adopt was hotly debated within the N-CF, with arguments being put forward for both sides. In the end the N-CF adopted an absolutist position, though acknowledged that, for all sorts of reasons but particularly ones of personal conscience and belief, not all members would want to follow this path. Also conscientious objectors sometimes changed their minds: John Brocklesby began as an alternativist, prepared to do what he felt might be work of national importance but, following his experience on what was known as the Home Office Scheme, adopted an absolutist position.

Chapter 3

Tribunals

'The Tribunals ... seem to take the view that a conscientious objector, whatever his statement of belief, is a person to be rebuked, bullied, and condemned.'

the *Tribunal*

In January 1916 when Parliament was discussing the terms of the Military Service Bill and the wording of the 'conscience clause', it was decided that those seeking exemption on grounds of conscientious objection would have to apply to, and appear before, tribunals. These tribunals would then assess the sincerity and validity of the applicant's beliefs and decide on the outcome – whether or not the conscientious objector should be exempted from military service. It was a mighty responsibility to put on tribunals, and turned out to be one that they were ill equipped to handle.

By March 1916 there were 2,086 local tribunals in Britain – 1,805 in England and Wales and 281 in Scotland. Corresponding to local authority regions, tribunals had first been used while registration and the Derby Scheme were in operation and they carried on after conscription was introduced. Tribunals were under the aegis of the Local Government Board, the government department responsible for overseeing all aspects of local government.

As well as local tribunals, there were also 83 appeal tribunals (68 in England and Wales and 15 in Scotland) and 1 central appeal tribunal. An applicant who was not satisfied with the outcome of a local tribunal could lodge an appeal with an appeal tribunal and then possibly to the central tribunal. The central tribunal itself often issued directions or pronouncements to local and appeal tribunals.

Intolerant and partial

All applications for exemption, not just those from conscientious objectors, went before tribunals although it is likely that conscientious objectors caused the greatest problems not least because tribunals had no previous experience whatsoever in dealing with matters of conscience. When the Military Service Bill was passing through Parliament, sympathetic MPs such as Philip Snowden and Charles Trevelyan had raised their concerns that tribunals would not be able to assess a man's conscience and had expressed fears that at a time of war with casualties as high as they were, tribunal members would not be able to remain unprejudiced. The general public saw conscientious objectors as shirkers, cowards and traitors; there was little reason to suppose that tribunal members would be any different. During a debate in the House of Commons on 19 January 1916, Quaker MP Edmund Harvey had suggested that COs should have their own special tribunals, while R.L. Outhwaite moved an amendment that COs should make a statement of their conscientious objection on oath before two JPs. Snowden supported the amendment though felt it should be made before a local tribunal, Snowden stating that 'they had not heard how they [the government] expect tribunals to discover whether an applicant has a conscientious objection or not'. The proposed amendments were rejected.

In the end, the task of assessing the sincerity of a conscientious objector was left to the discretion of the local tribunals. The local authorities – rural, district and borough councils – were responsible for appointing members of the tribunals and arranging the facilities. In a circular sent round to local authorities Mr Walter Long, President of the Local Government Board, advised that:

While care must be taken that the man who shirks his duty to his country does not find unworthy shelter behind this provision, every consideration should be given to the man whose objection generally rests on religious or moral convictions. Whatever may be the views of members of the Tribunal, they must interpret the Act in an impartial and tolerant spirit. Difference of convictions must not bias judgment. The local authority, in making their appointments to the Tribunal, should bear in mind that the Tribunal will have to hear, amongst the applicants, those made on the ground of conscientious objections. Men who apply on this ground should be able to feel that they are being judged by a Tribunal that will deal fairly with their cases.

Long went on to advise that the exemption should be the 'minimum required to meet the conscientious scruples of the applicant', and importantly that 'there may be exceptional cases in which the genuine convictions and the circumstances are such that neither exemption from combatant service nor a conditional exemption will adequately meet the case. Absolute exemption can be granted in these cases if the Tribunals are fully satisfied of the facts' and that tribunals could give absolute exemption if they were certain of the facts.

On the face of it this was a very liberal-minded approach but in practice tribunals were rarely 'impartial', 'tolerant' or 'fair'. Instead, the experience of most COs was that tribunals were bullying, prejudiced and intolerant: within a very short time it was clear that most tribunal members had little understanding of conscientious objectors – and certainly no sympathy for these men of military age who refused to fight. When Councillor Hopwood on Shaw tribunal, Lancashire, addressed the CO in front of him with the words: 'A man who would not defend his country or womankind is a coward and a cad. You are nothing but a shivering mass of unwholesome fat!' he was expressing what most tribunal members believed. Interestingly, the CO to whom Hopwood addressed this comment was a highly esteemed research scientist and member of one of the British Association's research committees. To be fair, tribunals were no respecters of class: they were capable of being just as rude and offensive to a nervous young farm labourer with deeply held pacifist principles and frequently were.

'When conscription was introduced there was the provision of tribunals to which we should go. They were not very sympathetic and were often rather crude in their attitude towards us, a thing one could understand when a nation was at war and there were not many who were exempted on the grounds that their convictions were sincere.'

Fenner Brockway

Part of the problem lay with the make-up of the tribunals. According to Quaker John Graham, who worked closely with conscientious objectors, attended tribunals and, as a Quaker chaplain, visited COs in prison, tribunals were made up mainly of 'elderly local magnates or tradesmen, often with a Labour man, known to be in favour of the war'. Occasionally, there was a woman on the tribunal, although according to Graham, who later wrote a history of the CO movement – *Conscription and Conscience* (1922), they were 'generally fiercer than the men'. Some members were justices of the peace, but most had no legal knowledge or experience and virtually no insight into the beliefs and principles of conscientious objectors. At a time when war was raging and men were dying in their thousands on the Western Front, tribunal members believed it was a man's duty to help the country and their fellow men; they simply could not understand why any man would refuse to do so on grounds of conscience.

Military representatives, appointed by the War Office, also attended tribunals and were a major barrier to fairness and impartiality. They were usually retired army officers or recruitment officers. They were not tribunal members and could not vote on outcomes but nevertheless they wielded considerable influence, advising tribunals and effectively acting as 'recruiting agents'. According to John Graham, the military representative:

> was an emissary of the War Office, a standing counsel against every application. Through always being there, often sitting at the same table as members of the Tribunal, and being akin in sympathies, these men dominated weak Tribunals. They were treated with a deference not granted to their opponents … They were generally in khaki, and often used their position to browbeat and intimidate applicants.

Significantly, military representatives as well as conscientious objectors had the right of appeal.

Applications

Another problem may also have been the sheer numbers of COs who appeared before the tribunals. Though they were only a small percentage of those who enlisted, it is probable no one had any idea just how many men would take a stand against conscription and military service. The War Office began sending out call-up papers –

War Office Form W3236 – in February 1916. At this point conscientious objectors had to decide whether to ignore their call-up and wait to be arrested for desertion, or whether to make a formal application for exemption on grounds of conscience. About 1,200 conscientious objectors flatly refused to apply to tribunals on the grounds that they did not recognise the government's right to tell them what to do. Given that under the Act all eligible men were 'deemed' to have enlisted, they were arrested and handed over to the army.

Most COs did apply for exemption. In March 1916, commenting on the fact that the first arrests were taking place, the N-CF began publishing its newsletter, the *Tribunal*, something *The Times* reported as the N-CF having added an official organ to its 'mischievous activities'.

In its first issue on 8 March, the *Tribunal*, which was edited by W.J. Chamberlain, stated that the N-CF needed to challenge the administration of the Military Service Act: 'The act recognises conscience and calls upon the conscientious objector to lay his case before Tribunals. Accordingly, some 10,000 members of the No-Conscription Fellowship and other bodies have sent in claims for exemption'. Written applications flooded into tribunals.

One was from Walter Ayles, prospective Labour candidate for East Bristol. He was an ILP member and on the N-CF's national committee. Applying for absolute exemption, he stated:

I am a Christian and a Socialist. Believing in the Gospels, I claim the right to interpret them according to my mind and conscience … I am profoundly convinced that the work of war is opposed to their teaching … I cannot and will not kill. I spend my life in an endeavour to save lives that are being beaten and destroyed in social and industrial warfare. I must continue to do that … I cannot … engage in the work of killing but must use all the energies I possess in an endeavour to bring the war to a successful and speedy end …

Fenner Brockway's application stressed his socialist beliefs:

my Socialism is based on a belief in the sacredness of human life … If this belief is to find expression in modern civilisation, the social order must be reconstructed … (1) to encourage what is best in human life instead of degrading it, and (2) to express the principle of co-operation instead of competition. War is the antitheses of

Socialism. It destroys human life and denies the unity of humanity. To participate in war would be to outrage my conscientious and most deeply held convictions. I cannot do it.

For J.H. Hudson, also a member of the N-CF's national committee:

all war is immoral ... In this war ... I am so convinced of the shameful betrayal of the common people of the world by their statesmen and rules in the preparation for, and the prosecution of this war, that I believe it to be my duty to the workers, to the International Brotherhood, and to my country, to stand firmly against this war ... I will neither excuse the war, nor support it by arms, nor accept it in any function which ... is offered to me as a bargain or alternative to military service ...

According to his granddaughter Angharad, David Thomas helped other local conscientious objectors to prepare for their tribunals as well as appearing before his own tribunal. His statement, dated 2 May 1916, explained his position:

I am opposed to the settlement of international disputes by the exercise of physical force, as the result of war does not determine which side was right, it only shows which side was the stronger. I believe the present war, and indeed most wars, to be the natural result of the constant struggle between the Powers for dominion and gain – which I have always opposed. My efforts have been directed towards strengthening the bonds of international friendship, and I shall continue my efforts in that direction, come what may. I believe that course to be the only one that is consistent with the spirit of Christians. I am conscientiously opposed to everything that destroys human life. I know nothing in the world that is so precious as human life, and I cannot feel justified, under any circumstances, in destroying men's lives for the sake of anything of less value. I feel it to be the duty of every man to devote himself entirely to his country's service and I have endeavoured to do so for many years wherever I thought I could be more useful. I am willing to help my country today, but I will not help her to do what is wrong. I cannot place my service in any capacity at the disposal of a War Government to be utilised by it and to further its own purposes.

Swamped by applications such as these, it is perhaps not surprising that tribunals felt overwhelmed and confused.

Appearing before the tribunal
Having sent in an application, COs were then called to appear before their local tribunal. Hearings were open to the public, including the press, unless tribunals decided otherwise. Usually, observers or members of the public were friends and family of objectors, who often found it hard to remain silent when tribunal members behaved in a particularly unacceptable manner. And for applicants the fact that their deeply held beliefs were being misunderstood was frustrating and sometimes upsetting.

Fred Murfin was a printer before the war, working in Louth, Lincolnshire. He became a pacifist, joined the N-CF and applied for absolute exemption. In 1965, when he was in his 70s, he wrote an account of his experiences as a CO, entitled 'Prisoners for Peace':

> The Tribunals were open to the public and sympathisers attended in numbers, often commenting aloud. I received my first notice on March 8th, 1916, 'the case to be heard on March 13th at 4.30 at the Tottenham Town Hall, North London.' When I arrived, a case was being heard in camera, and when it was over they tried to keep the public out. There was uproar, and the Tribunal was adjourned. My case was eventually heard on March 23rd. It was a terrible ordeal for anyone sensitive; I found it very trying. How does one feel when trying, in public, to convince people, who are out to misconstrue everything one says, that because of one's religious convictions – no matter what the consequences – no war service is possible?

Fred Murfin's experience was not at all unusual. Baffled by conscientious objectors and feeling a duty to bring men into the army, most tribunals treated objectors with disdain and rudeness, COs finding themselves on the receiving end of questions and comments that were at best dismissive and at worst downright aggressive and bullying. Although tribunals varied in their approach towards conscientious objectors, by and large it was clear that they had no sympathy or understanding of their position. Far from being impartial, tribunal members frequently described COs to their face as 'cads', 'cowards' and 'shirkers'. Anti-conscientious objector prejudice was strikingly obvious. An applicant who appeared before the West Glamorgan appeal tribunal and stated that he was a member of the N-CF was told: 'You belong to one of the most pernicious bodies in the country. Its members are going all over the place distilling poison, and are greater enemies to Britain than the Germans.' The chairman of the Wirral tribunal made his views perfectly clear when he declared: 'I wish the Government had not put this clause about conscientious objectors in the Act at all. I don't agree with it myself.' And the chairman of Ashton-under-Lyne tribunal asked another applicant: 'Is it the conscience that makes cowards of us all that you are suffering from?'

Examples of this sort of partiality and bullying were legion, and the *Tribunal* consistently reported on them, sometimes with considerable wit, which was very charitable given how N-CF members and other COs were being treated. One example occurred in March 1916 at the Holborn tribunal in London when a member of the tribunal asked the applicant, who was a member of the N-CF, a series of inane questions including 'What time do you get up?', 'What time do you go to bed?', 'What exercise do you take?' and 'What do you do on Sunday?'. The 'bemused' CO answered the questions and was then finally asked how often he took a bath. The CO replied 'Oh, quite often', to which a member of the tribunal replied: 'Judging by your appearance you don't look as if you did.' The N-CF, after some research, established that the person who had asked these questions was in fact a Mr A.W. Gamage, owner of Gamages, a well-known department store in central London. Writing humorously about the incident in April 1916, the *Tribunal* commented that at first they could not believe that a person of Gamage's position 'could sink to such depths of vulgar impertinence' but now they knew the truth, 'we can only assume that his keen business instinct got the better of his sense of decency and that he was probably endeavouring to sell the applicant something in the cycle or bath line!', a very witty response to quite inappropriate behaviour.

Some tribunal members focused on undermining the views of religious objectors, though by so doing they often displayed their own ignorance. In one instance at Clowne tribunal, the chairman asked an objector whether he had 'read where He went into the Temple and lashed them all out?' The applicant responded: 'But He did not kill them' to which the chairman replied: 'No, but he probably would have done if he had had a gun.' In another exchange, at Sandown tribunal, a Colonel Gordon quoted Christ's words: 'I came not to bring peace but a sword.' The objector responded by quoting the Sermon on the Mount – 'love your enemies, bless them that curse you … pray for them that despitefully use you', to which Colonel Gordon responded: 'But surely, that was personal, not national.'

> **The military representative's little joke**
> *'At Salford a conscientious objector said he was a vegetarian. The military representative said they were not asking for cannibals to eat the enemy; they wanted fighters!'*
>
> the *Tribunal*, 15 March 1916

Questioning

Typically, members addressed a series of questions to objectors appearing before them. These were intended to be searching questions aimed at establishing an objector's sincerity but were in themselves often farcical. A standard question, which became notorious, was what an objector would do if a German attempted to rape the objector's sister or mother, to which Lytton Strachey, a leading light of the Bloomsbury Group, who applied for conscientious objection in 1916, is alleged to have replied, 'I would attempt to interpose myself'.

Only a few tribunal records have survived but some COs or their friends made detailed notes of questions and answers. In his memoirs, John Brocklesby gives a very full account of his hearing, including the responses of tribunal members. He was summoned to appear with other COs at the Doncaster tribunal. They arrived early, went to have their hair cut and then 'climbed the dingy stone staircase at the Union Office', where the hearing was to take place. Brocklesby was called first:

Clerk:	You have a conscientious objection to killing?
B:	Yes, sir.
Clerk:	Would you retaliate if you were attacked?
B:	No, sir.
Clerk:	If I were to smite you on one cheek would you turn the other?
B:	It is our Christian duty, sir.

Clerk:	But give me a plain answer, yes or no. If I were to knock one of your teeth out, wouldn't you try to knock two of mine out?
B:	The question is hypothetical. One cannot say what one would do in the heat of the moment.
Clerk:	I will put another hypothetical question. If you were attacked by Germans would you kill to save your own life?
B:	In view of the Sixth Commandment, it is better to be killed than to kill.
Clerk:	But if the Germans were to arrive at Conisborough and attack your Mother?
B:	The case is hypothetical; I believe God would provide a way of escape before things got so far.
Clerk:	But it happened in Belgium.
B:	Yes, but the menfolk ran away and left their women to the tender mercies of the Germans.
Clerk:	But suppose ... that you were really cornered and there was no way of escape. If you were attacked by Germans with bayonets and you had a revolver, would you shoot?
B:	No sir, it would be a happy release from this miserable world.
	(The Clerk grunts and throws up the sponge.)

At this point someone else took over the questioning and asked him about his membership of the N-CF during which Brocklesby made it clear that he would not accept any exemption from the tribunal that would assist the military war effort. The response was:

Baker:	Well now, if you are determined to refuse whatever this tribunal may be prepared to award, why do you come here?
B:	We merely come as an acknowledgement of the concession made to the conscientious objectors by the government.
Baker:	Now, sir, answer my question.
B:	I have answered it as well as I can.
	(Chairman agrees.)

Baker:	Well then, if the Germans were attacking Doncaster, if you could save the lives of some women and children, would you do so?
B:	I would try to save life, but not by taking life.
Baker:	Would you not shoot any Germans?
B.	No, sir.
Baker:	Would you knock any down?
B:	Perhaps.
	(Snort from apoplectic member.)
Chairman:	If you would not take life to save the lives of hundreds of women and children, you would be responsible for their deaths. (Smiles and gazes triumphantly around the tribunal.)
A Member:	Would you be prepared to take non-combatant service, say in a munitions factory or minesweeping?
B:	No, sir, they would not let me sweep English mines as well as German mines.
Clerk:	It seems as if he has an objection to doing anything that will take him into danger.
B:	It is very difficult to bring evidence to prove a conscientious objection; one can only prove it by suffering for it. I am prepared to die for my principles. I am fighting for the principle of freedom of conscience for every Englishman and I am prepared to die for my principles. It would be a pity if, while there are so many thousands who are ready to die for their country, there are not some who are prepared to die for higher principles.
Baker:	Are you a local preacher?
B:	Yes.
Baker:	Well, you had better go and preach somewhere else. (Laughter.)
Chairman:	We will forward to you our decision.

According to Brocklesby, the local press covered his hearing under the 'derisive' headline: 'CO says he had rather be killed than kill', something which in 1916 Brocklesby says was 'considered the height of absurdity, as well as the limit of shirking one's duty'.

Not all objectors were questioned at such length. Tribunal hearings, at local level anyway, were often rushed through so that on many occasions an applicant was not given the opportunity to explain his views. This happened to Harold Bing:

> When the Act was passed and the date was fixed for applications for exemption on any grounds, health, business, conscientious objection or anything else ... I sent in my application to the local tribunal and in due course I was summoned to appear before it. The hearing was rather a farce. My name was called. I appeared before the tribunal. My father and one or two other friends offered as witnesses to speak on my behalf if necessary. The chairman of the tribunal, after one or two formal questions, asked me how old I was. I said I was 18 years of age. He said 'Well, in that case you're not old enough to have a conscience. Case dismissed.' My father got up to protest at such summary treatment but the chairman called 'Next case, next case, next case' and the clerk explained that there was no next case, I was the last case to be heard that day and so the chairman and fellow members of the tribunal got up and left the room leaving my father still protesting ... In fact the whole case was so casually treated that they'd not even noticed that they'd not got the original testimonials; they'd only got copies. They didn't even ask for the originals. This farcical treatment led to considerable concern on the part of a number of people who were there and a number of them signed a statement expressing their view of the inadequacy and complete illegality [of the proceedings] ...

Exemption
Conscientious objectors could apply for one of three different kinds of exemption from their local tribunal: absolute exemption, without any conditions at all, which clearly is what most COs were aiming for; conditional exemption from military service, namely exemption from military service conditional on doing non-military work of 'national importance'; or exemption from combatant duties only, which meant they were prepared to join the army but in a non-combatant role only. Many COs, when putting in their applications for exemption, outlined what it was they were prepared to do, choices that were influenced by whether they were 'absolutists' or 'alternativists'.

For their part tribunals had four choices. They could refuse an application completely; they could grant exemption from combatant service only; grant exemption conditional on the applicant doing work of national importance; and give absolute exemption, with conditions. COs who got an exemption, on whatever grounds, received a certificate of exemption, which could be reviewed at any time.

It was extremely rare for tribunals to grant absolute exemption to any conscientious objector. They were legally allowed to do so – the Military Service Act stated that any certificate of exemption could be absolute, conditional or temporary – and the circular sent to tribunals from Mr Walter Long, President of the Local Government Board, had clearly stated that although exemptions should be the 'minimum required', it had also clearly said that there might be 'exceptional cases' where 'genuine convictions' of an applicant might be such absolute exemption would be the only option. Even so, it was obvious that most tribunals had no wish whatsoever to grant absolute exemption and went to considerable lengths to avoid doing so. Some tribunals explicitly refused to follow directives. Durham appeal tribunal stated that 'We are not bound by any statement made by Members of Parliament or any circular issued by the Local Government Board' and many other tribunals, whether they believed it or not, told applicants that they were not allowed to grant absolute exemption. Some tribunals, including Falmouth, Helston, Bromley, Doncaster and Swansea, defied regulations and held hearings in private, keeping the public out. Military representatives contributed to the violation of rules and frequently overstepped their remit, not least by bullying and spreading misinformation. At Sheffield the military representative told an objector that the only way to absolute exemption was death and at Seaton Delaval tribunal, following a consultation with the military representative, the chairman told an applicant that he would be shot if he refused non-combatant service. There were also cases of military representatives tearing up certificates of exemption. This happened to Henry Sargent: his tribunal was granted exemption conditional on doing work of national importance but the military representative appealed and Sargent was ordered to report for military service.

Fundamentally, tribunal members were as prejudiced against conscientious objectors as the public at large. They did not believe that objectors should be let off and they were encouraged in this by the military representatives, who had specifically been instructed to get as many men into the army as possible. Tribunal members did not understand the depth of principles held by conscientious objectors nor in many cases were they prepared to accept carefully thought out personal statements, membership of anti-war or peace organisations or accounts of well-established pacifist views as evidence of a sincere conscientious objection to war.

One of the difficulties, prejudice apart, was that tribunals focused on a narrow but literal definition of the Military Service Act, namely that an applicant had to prove a conscientious objection to combatant service, and if that was so then that was all they had to do: they did not need to grant absolute exemption, nor if they were disinclined grant exemption conditional on doing work of national importance although many did use this latter category. As a result, no more than 400 out of a total of 16,000 COs were given absolute exemption, most of them Quakers. The fact that the majority of COs who appeared before tribunals could prove their anti-war or pacifist beliefs cut little ice with tribunals; essentially, they either could not or would not recognise the sincerity of the objectors.

The *Tribunal* reported many examples of extraordinary exemptions. Brentford tribunal refused to give absolute exemption to conscientious objectors but they gave it to members of the Brewery Company, who the tribunal considered were doing work of 'national importance'. Southwark tribunal gave six months exemption to twenty-one men employed by the Harmsworth Press on *Home Chat, Comic Cuts* and other popular magazines – no doubt because the tribunal deemed these to be of national importance. And at Market Bosworth, the tribunal gave exemption to all the men in the local hunt.

Bias towards religious objectors
By and large religious objectors were treated better than those whose stand was political or moral. According to Wilfred Littleboy, an absolutist from Birmingham:

Well then, 'Will you March too, or wait till March 2?' as the posters went in 1916 – that was the date when the conscription Act first came in, and special tribunals were set up to which people might apply … Their first duty was to be quite sure that the conviction that was claimed by applicants was really genuine, and there was very little difficulty for members of most of the Society of Friends: it was recognised and accepted that would be the case. But those whose claims were on political or moral grounds, rather than religious, had a much more difficult time in proving their convictions before tribunals.

This point was proved on many occasions. In Burnley on 27 March 1916, an applicant stated to the tribunal that he was a conscientious objector because he was a socialist. Following a brief exchange the application was refused, the chairman stating that the applicant could not claim 'to be a Socialist and a conscientious objector'. When two members of the N-CF national committee appeared before Birmingham tribunal, one of them, A. Barratt Brown, had his Quaker stand recognised, while Will Chamberlain, editor of the *Tribunal*, who was a socialist, had his application rejected.

Sometimes tribunals specifically stated that they would not grant exemption to political objectors, as Stephen Winsten found. He felt he could not label himself as either a religious or political objector so, acting on advice from Fenner Brockway, asked Aylmer Maude, Tolstoy's biographer, to write him a witness statement. In his letter Maude explained that pacifism to Winsten was 'native even if he can't justify it or explain it and you'll never get him to fight'. Maude further stated that Winsten would be a 'nuisance' to the army. In response the military representative merely asked Winsten that given that Britain had provided him with work as a teacher, didn't he think that Winsten owed something to the country. In his interview with the IWM, Winsten said:

> That letter didn't influence him ... because he thought it was one conchie supporting another conchie ... He meant that I was a dirty cad ... I was then teaching in the roughest school in London and teaching according to my principles ... so I said to him, 'It is because I *love* England sir, that I'm willing to serve in any position and do a service which I don't think you would ever do.' 'Well,' he said, 'I think we'll put you down as a political objector. And therefore you can't get exemption. We can only give it to religious [objectors].

Winsten, who had anglicised his original name Samuel Weinstein, was one of the 'Whitechapel Boys', a group of young Jewish writers in the East End before the First World War. Following his tribunal and subsequent arrest, he served time in Bedford and Reading prisons and later wrote a book of poetry, *Chains* (1920) based on his experiences.

On another occasion, the Oxford appeal tribunal heard applications from thirty Oxford undergraduates who, according to John Graham, were 'as fine and brave a group as I have ever seen, whose sincerity was written on every face and in every attitude'. All were sent into non-combatant duties in the army; only one, a Quaker, was exempted conditional on working with the FAU.

The bias towards religious objectors was reinforced in June 1916 when the central tribunal advised local and appeal tribunals that in its view only religious objectors could legitimately claim exemption on grounds of conscientious objection and socialist and other political objectors could not be considered 'genuine' conscientious objectors. The central tribunal also said that the tribunals should take the age of a conscientious objector into consideration when making a decision, implying that, as in the case of John Brocklesby, a young man could not be expected to have a well thought out conscience.

Despite protests against this from the Joint Advisory Committee, which led to a clarification from the Local Government Board stating that conscientious objection could be 'moral' as well as religious, tribunals continued pretty well to follow their courses of action.

Tribunals did not only have real difficulties with recognising political objectors, they also failed to understand the complexity of conscientious objection, which according to the individual could range from a profound Christian belief in the sanctity of human life through to the rejection of conscription and killing as a civil liberties issue and a refusal to allow the State to dictate a man's actions. In an interview with the IWM, Howard Marten described how his first local tribunal was:

> pretty hostile. They were men of not very great depth of vision or understanding, and although I wouldn't say that I was a complete absolutist, a do-nothing, I wasn't prepared to do anything under military direction, or to be exempted in a very restricted way. I think people get the impression that it was only that people wouldn't fight. It was something more than that; it was an objection to having one's life directed by an outside authority.

Wilfred Littleboy came from a long line of Quakers. As he described in an interview with the IWM, when war began what had been 'an inherited conviction' became a 'living personal conviction' as he prepared himself to refuse military service. An active Quaker – he became an elder in 1912 – and involved with the N-CF, he worked as an accountant in Birmingham. In 1916 he appeared before his local tribunal in Birmingham, where Neville Chamberlain, then mayor of Birmingham, was chairman. According to Littleboy, Chamberlain was '...within limits, entirely considerate. "Couldn't you do so and so?" and "You're an accountant, couldn't you go into the office of a munitions factory? You'd be paid as an accountant." Well, I was surprised that a person of his intelligence asked a question of that kind because the answer, to me at any rate, seemed so obvious.'

To Wilfred Littleboy the reasons were obvious; he was not prepared, as a matter of conscience, to work within a munitions factory that produced the weapons of war, even if it was as an accountant, but the tribunal members failed to understand why a man who had been exempted from actually picking up a gun would refuse alternative work as an accountant, albeit in a munitions factory. Chamberlain adjourned the case for one month but when Littleboy returned to the tribunal he continued his objection. This time the chairman was much harsher and berated Littleboy for his views. As a result Littleboy found it far easier to say no: 'It's much easier to say no to a person who's losing his temper than to someone who is being conciliatory.' He was refused exemption and posted to a non-combatant unit.

British Prussianism
Sympathetic MPs and particularly Philip Snowden did everything they could to raise the issue of tribunal abuse in the House of Commons, asking questions on an almost daily basis. On 22 March Snowden made a long speech to the House, in which he provided evidence that the Military Service Act was not being 'administered in a fair and judicial manner, and that its provisions are being most flagrantly violated by those who have had imposed on them the responsibility of its administration', namely the tribunals. He cited fifty-four cases of abuse, not just towards conscientious objectors but also to applicants seeking exemption on other grounds. According to Snowden, these were only one-twentieth of the cases that had been brought to his attention, many of them by the N-CF. Many of the cases referred to

men being threatened, abused or even kidnapped and forced into the army by recruiting and military officers. Other cases that he mentioned referred to conscientious objectors whose application forms for exemption were being sent too late to allow for preparation for a tribunal. Similarly, he cited cases where conscientious objectors, having appeared before local tribunals, were then refused the right to appeal, in violation of the law. Describing the treatment of conscientious objectors by tribunals as 'nothing short of an outrage and a public scandal', he referred to many examples of tribunals heaping 'scorn and insults' on applicants, such as a member of the Oldbury tribunal saying to an applicant, 'It seems to me there are two things you possess – cowardice and insolence', and the chairman of Nairn tribunal, who described conscientious objectors in front of him as 'the most awful pack that ever walked this earth!'. In another example, at Gower tribunal, the military representative asked an applicant if he had ever been in a lunatic asylum, called another applicant a traitor and added that, 'He was only fit to be on a point of a German bayonet.'

This speech and another similar one that Philip Snowden made to the House of Commons, by which time Snowden said he was receiving seventy-five letters a day complaining about tribunals, were printed in a penny pamphlet entitled 'British Prussianism: The Scandal of the Tribunals', which was widely circulated. His evidence was picked by the *Daily Chronicle*, which published a leading article criticising the workings of the tribunals. The Bishop of Oxford also wrote a letter to *The Times* advising tribunals to be 'more respectful where there is good evidence of conscientious objection', a view also expressed strongly and courageously in a letter from the Bishop of Lincoln, which was published in *The Times* on 4 April 1916 and in which he said:

> As I read of the handling of conscientious objectors by some local tribunals, I am visited by some painful fears. The Act of Parliament under which these men were recruited provides in explicit terms that the conscientious objector to war is to be exempt from service ... I have no wish to screen cowards or shirkers ... but that there are among us conscientious objectors, all agree ... Such a man may be useless for war, but he may be a useful citizen ... Is the nation, in its military zeal slipping into the old vices of intolerance and persecution? Conscience is a sacred thing. Is private judgement to be swept wholly aside in time of war ... 'What chance would Christ

have today?' wrote Mabel Dearmer [novelist and pacifist] bitterly from Serbia: 'Crucifixion would be a gentle death for such a dangerous lunatic.' ... it is perilous to trample on conscience; we must not try to deprive the honest objector of the protection secured to him by the law of the land.

Needless to say, on the days following this, a considerable number of letters were published in *The Times* criticising the Bishop of Lincoln for his views.

Despite Snowden's efforts and any publicity given to the behaviour of tribunals, the British public was for more concerned with the ever-increasing casualty lists and the sufferings of soldiers in the trenches. No one really cared how tribunals were treating conscientious objectors, who were after all seen by most of the public as at best cranks and at worst cowardly traitors. As a result the tribunals continued to be what John Graham called 'painful places' for COs.

Outcomes
Figures for tribunal decisions vary but John Graham, who used the records of the Conscientious Objectors' Information Bureau, states that out of the approximately 16,000 men who appeared in front of tribunals, only about 200 (some sources say 400) conscientious objectors received absolute exemption from military service. Some 6,500 conscientious objectors were given exemption conditional on doing 'alternative service' by finding work of national importance. They included 1,600 men whose conditions meant working with the FAU, the Quakers' War Victims' Relief Committee or the Royal Army Medical Corps. About 5,500 were given non-combatant status and were sent to the Non-Combatant Corps (NCC), a special army unit formed in 1916. About 2,500 conscientious objectors had their applications dismissed, resulting in them being sent forcibly into the army for combat duties. Some 6,000 of those who appeared before tribunals refused to accept the tribunals' decisions.

Chapter 4

Alternative Service

'Thank God from the bottom of my heart for the inestimable privilege of being allowed to try and patch up the results of this ghastly mistake.'
Corder Catchpool

Most coverage of First World War conscientious objectors focuses on the absolutists, those who refused to compromise with the Military Service Act and who were not prepared to accept the decision of tribunals. Their stories are dramatic and their resistance and consequences unprecedented within the peace movement, although paralleled by the courage and determination of the militant suffragettes who preceded them.

There were however a few thousand conscientious objectors – the alternativists – who were prepared to take alternative service either in non-combatant units within the military, or in civilian occupations specified by tribunals and considered to be work of national importance. Their stories are not necessarily as dramatic or trailblazing as those of their absolutist comrades but their contribution to the CO movement was significant inasmuch as it proved that conscientious objectors could make a valuable contribution to a society at war, without having to pick up arms and kill anyone.

Absolute or alternative?

There was quite a lot of debate among conscientious objectors, particularly within the N-CF as to whether it was right or wrong to take 'alternative service'. Writing in the *Tribunal*, 11 May 1916, Clifford Allen, who was an absolutist, made his personal position clear but called for tolerance for those who were not absolutists, reminding his readers that conscience must always be a personal matter:

I, personally, cannot accept Alternative Service. Knowing that this is a Military Service Act for men of military age, and not a National Service Act for men and women of all ages ... The strain through which we are all passing is enough to test the wisest of us, but it is just as essential that we should remain tolerant ... There is a tendency ... to define men as conscientious objectors according to whether they are or are not prepared to accept alternative civil service. Surely this is a grave error. Have we not all along said that the individual himself can be the only judge of his own conscience? ... The Convention, by an overwhelming majority, declared against alternative service. Some men are hesitating to take this service solely through loyalty to the Fellowship. This is entirely misguided. Such loyalty to the Fellowship will only result in the gravest disloyalty to the individual conscience ... I urge upon all my fellow members, and upon our Branches not to let this question of alternative service raise difficulties ... Let those of us who cannot accept it honour those who have no such objection ...

One who did decide to take alternative service was Bernard Noel Langdon-Davies. Previously a member of the UDC, he subsequently helped to found, and was secretary of, the National Council against Conscription, later the National Council for Civil Liberties. The Council co-operated with the N-CF, producing information leaflets, keeping a watchful eye on the actions taken under the Defence of the Realm Act and assisting COs applying for exemption. In Langdon-Davies' own account, published in *We Did Not Fight* (1935), he describes how he had to make a series of decisions: 'whether to follow the herd in support of the war, whether to accept or oppose conscription and whether to accept alternative service'. Influenced by Norman Angell, he became a pacifist, a position that he maintained for the rest of his life, and in due course appeared in front of a tribunal as a conscientious objector. The tribunal directed him into non-combatant service, he appealed and his appeal tribunal granted him exemption 'conditional on doing work of national importance'. In Langdon-Davies' opinion, 'the final decision for conscientious objectors did not rest with Tribunals or Committees, or, except in a very material sense, with anyone or anything but themselves'. Feeling that 'if I went to prison, my work for the Council and possibly the Council itself were going to cease and that the support of my family and the proper education of my children would be sacrificed to my desire to approximate to consistency', he opted for alternative service. Despite his impressive qualifications, he was put to work as a baker, working with the Bermondsey Co-operative Bakery, a job that he enjoyed, that he considered was important and which also allowed him time to continue with his anti-war work.

As Langdon-Davies and Clifford Allen described, conscience is a personal matter. The reasons why many conscientious objectors accepted alternative civil work varied. Some, such as such as Quakers, felt they had a duty to do what they could to alleviate the dreadful suffering caused by war; others felt they could not put their families to dire financial straits by taking a stand that would inevitably lead to prison, while there were others who thought that if they could do something useful, provided it did not clash with their deeply held principles, it was for them the right choice. Knowing where to draw their personal line in terms of involvement was a dilemma for objectors, whose every action was determined by their personal consciences. Even then decisions were not always cast in stone; as war progressed, some who had been alternativists shifted ground to an absolutist position and vice versa.

Work of 'national importance'
Some 6,500 conscientious objectors were granted exemption from military service conditional on them finding work of 'national importance'. The COs had to find the work, which had to be approved by the tribunal. If a CO failed to find employment that met the tribunal's requirements, his status could be changed and he would most likely be sent into the army, either as a combatant or non-combatant. At least 4,000 COs accepted the decision and could be found working in hospitals and farms around Britain, or helping the wounded and refugees in France and Belgium.

Whether the tribunals wanted to or not, they had been instructed that they were empowered to grant exemption from military service conditional on the conscientious objector doing work of national importance. Defining work of national importance was not easy, particularly when applied to conscientious objectors who, by definition, would not take up occupations linked to the war effort, such as making munitions. The question was debated in the House of Commons and a Committee on Work of National Importance was set up by the Board of Trade on 28 March 1916. Known usually as the Pelham Committee after its first chairman, H.W. Pelham, its remit was advisory: it informed tribunals about suitable occupations and aimed to help to bring workers and work together. Pacifist MP Edmund Harvey was one of the Committee members.

In April 1916 the committee produced a list of suitable civilian occupations, which it considered should be seen as work of national importance. These were agriculture, including labouring, market gardening and fruit growing, and making and repairing farming equipment; forestry; food supply, including working in mills and sugar refineries; shipping, including making and repairing ships; transport, including working on railways, canals and docks; mining; education; and 'public utility services', which covered working with the fire services, sanitation and jobs in hospitals, including mental hospitals. The committee circulated the list to tribunals and recommended that tribunals should approach them for advice if required.

According to John Graham, the Pelham Committee was the most satisfactory of all the bodies that the government set up. And from 1916 until the end of the war, it did help to place nearly 4,000 conscientious objectors in employment, including 1,400 Christadelphians. However, there were problems. For a start the committee was advisory only, not mandatory, and it could only advise if tribunals chose to consult it, which, certainly at first, most tribunals chose not to do. One of the problems was that tribunals were initially reluctant to grant conditional exemption, preferring instead to direct conscientious objectors into non-combatant services within the army. As a result in the first weeks after the Act, most conditional exemptions went to Quakers only. However, as time went on and married men joined single objectors from June 1916 tribunals began to make more use of the Pelham Committee.

Some tribunals also misunderstood the situation either deliberately or unwittingly. The clerk of the appeal court at Manchester thought the committee was extremely irritating and did not brief the chairman, Judge Mellor, with accurate information. As a result the chairman gave a number of conscientious objectors he thought were genuine: 'non-combatant service under the Pelham Committee', which was a technical contradiction in terms. As a result men who should have been sent into work, were sent into the army. Quaker John Graham put Judge Mellor straight and, to his credit, the chairman tried to correct the situation, recalling most of the men and directing them into 'work of national importance under the Pelham Committee'. A few however slipped through the net and could not be recalled from the army. John Graham wrote to the press describing the 'muddle' and outlining what was effectively a catch-22 situation:

> Yesterday I was permitted to visit a brave young fellow in the guardroom at Bury Barracks. He is a working man and his parents are dependent on him. He is … in conflict with the military authority and in danger of imminent court martial … He received from the Salford Hundred Appeal Tribunal at Manchester relief from combatant duties only, and was referred to the Pelham Committee … This decision recognizes the reality of his conscientious objection. It is, however, self-contradictory, for a man excused from combatant duties is still a soldier under military orders, while the Pelham Committee is formed to provide and organize occupations for those who are exempted conditionally on finding work of national importance. But here comes in the curious thing characteristic of the present muddle, all of whose confusions … tell against exemptions. The chairman and the clerk of this Tribunal have both refused to take any action whatever with the Pelham Committee towards carrying out the decision. They say they have nothing to do with it and … assert that they have no official cognizance of its existence, though in fact the clerk has received its circulars. The Pelham Committee, on their side, are only authorized to deal with cases sent to them by the Tribunals. Between these two the victim … falls to the ground; the decision becomes a mockery, the military take advantage of it and capture their man.

The problem might not have arisen if conscientious objectors had been allowed to remain in their pre-war occupations, particularly those who were doing what was actually listed as work of national importance, such as teaching. However, when it came to directing objectors into civilian work, tribunals were influenced by the idea of 'equal sacrifice': men in the trenches were suffering and had to make considerable personal sacrifices, therefore COs who had failed to respond to the call, should be prepared to make sacrifices and suffer also, a view that was solidly held by the right-wing press and most of the public. In fact, most conscientious objectors also, most of whom had considerable respect for the men in the trenches, would have agreed. However, it did mean that conscientious objectors, many of whom were highly skilled and could have made a more positive social contribution, were not allowed to stay where they were but were placed, in the main, into manual work. As a result, trained and experienced teachers were put to work in quarries and on the land, a waste of skill and talent but a decision solidly backed by the general public and most local authorities.

Work on the land
In a rather back-handed and unpleasant letter published in *The Times* in March 1916, a 'Chaplain to the Forces' suggested that tribunals should keep lists of conscientious objectors, or 'in better words men whose courage evidently goes by default' and inform farmers that these COs were available for employment on the land. In the letter writer's opinion this would prevent COs from 'living in comfort at home' and also meant there would be no need 'to call the women and girls of the country to do work for which we all admit they are but badly fitted'. It is a little difficult to know what upset the letter writer most: COs or land girls.

In fact many COs were put to work on the land. Some farmers were reluctant to employ conscientious objectors but others accepted them. Although the work was very different from what they had done before, many COs considered it was important, helping to increase food production, and several found they gained from the experience.

R.B. Scott worked on the land together with other conscientious objectors. The work was hard but the 'great compensation' was that it was in the open air. It was 'far from a holiday and it would be foolish to neglect the seamy side. A few weeks of wet, chaff-cutting, the mud and cold of winter, some twelve-hour days of harvesting and other trials of this kind are by no means pleasant …'. He enjoyed the companionship of the other COs, commenting on the comradeship that developed between men who had one thing in common: 'the hatred of war and the determination to have nothing to do with it'. He was also working with 'old men' and soldiers. Interestingly, he found that the soldiers 'were the more friendly and seemed to feel very little bitterness against us' but the same was not true of the older men who 'growled and cursed'. Like other COs in his situation, Scott was only too aware of the reasons why this should have been so: 'we should expect it when we consider the position of comparative safety in which we are placed'. Many COs who worked on the land felt their efforts made a vital contribution by enabling food production to continue when farm workers had gone to the front. There were others however who grappled with their conscience, fearing that their employment merely freed another man for the trenches.

COs also worked in a variety of other occupations: as bakers, in the mines, in welfare work, on the railways, in food production and in hospitals and what were then called asylums. One conscientious objector was given a job as an undertaker. A few were even kept in their original jobs, though this was unusual.

Unfit to teach

Letting a conscientious objector teach in schools was considered to be particularly unacceptable. In December 1916, during a meeting of the London Education Committee, it was decided by 16 votes to 9 that London County Council (LCC) schools would no longer employ as teachers conscientious objectors who had been exempted from military service conditional on doing work of national importance, and that teachers who had appealed for exemption on grounds of conscience and been found unfit for military service, would be given a month's notice. The Revd Scott Lidgett objected, saying that as a public body they should not penalise someone for exercising a legal right but he was overruled, one of the members of the committee stating that he 'would be no party to asking children whose fathers were at the front to sit in a class conducted by a conscientious objector', a view echoed in many other education committees and councils. Generally, it was felt that any teacher who was a CO would pollute the minds of young people in the classroom and infect them with anti-war views. Much the same attitude prevailed twenty years later during the Second World War when conscientious objectors were sacked from teaching positions.

David Thomas, who had been working as a primary teacher in Talysarn, North Wales, fell into this category. A socialist, local preacher and staunchly anti-war, he was well known locally for his anti-conscription and anti-war views.

Hardly surprisingly then, Thomas applied for absolute exemption and appeared before his local tribunal in Caernarvon on 28 April 1916. He was directed into non-combatant service. He appealed against the decision, asking that he should remain in his occupation as a teacher but the appeal tribunal, while recognising his sincerity, did not consider that he was entitled to any exemption other than combatant service. They added a rider that he had only been given the right of appeal because he had 'taken a prominent part in labour and social questions in the neighbourhood' and wanted to give him every opportunity of 'proving his case'. Thomas then moved onto the central tribunal, which in August 1916 granted exemption from combatant service and non-combatant service, provided he could find work of national importance that the tribunal approved within twenty-one days.

Thomas hoped to remain in his teaching post and applied to the Education Authority and the Pelham Committee for agreement that his existing work should be considered of national importance. He was though pretty well passed from pillar to post. Following a staff committee meeting, he was instructed to inform the central tribunal that the Education Authority 'do not consider his services indispensable to the efficient running of Talysarn School, but if the Central Tribunal considers that Mr Thomas is doing work of national importance while engaged at [the] school this Committee are prepared to retain him in their services'. The Pelham Committee acknowledged that the Education Authority were prepared to keep him in post but had no powers to make this happen; instead they stated that the decision had to rest with the central tribunal.

Needless to say, the central tribunal did not accept Thomas's request to continue as a teacher. In November 1916 – Thomas had successfully applied for an extension of time – the Pelham Committee advised Thomas that if he was not kept on as a teacher, he would need to find alternative work, adding that the central tribunal 'desire that the work should be at a distance of not less than 50 miles from your home', which was typical of the punitive conditions imposed on conscientious objectors. Most men were told they had to find work at least 25 miles away from their homes, which often meant a man on reduced pay having to try and support two homes.

Finding work was not easy. David Thomas wrote many letters, which are archived in Bangor University, applying for work but was consistently turned down. He wrote for a job with J. Crichton & Co., shipbuilders, and received a letter back saying, 'We have at the moment, no suitable employment to offer you' and received a similar response from the British Oil & Cake Mills Ltd. None of the letters refusing him a job mentioned his status as a CO but his granddaughter Angharad has little doubt this was the reason. One firm offered him heavy manual work connected with 'fertilizers or artificial manure' but, discovering the firm was connected to the munitions industry, David Thomas could not take the offer. Finally, in December 1916, he wrote to the committee telling them that he had been offered work as a farm labourer in Wrexham, which the central tribunal accepted.

Petty tyrannies
This sort of experience was not at all unusual. There were many examples of COs having considerable difficulty in finding work. Councils were not the only organisations that did not want to employ them. In June 1917 members of the East Hetton Colliery Lodge of the Durham Miners' Association passed a resolution stating that they were not prepared to allow any of their members to hold office who were conscientious objectors and in fact opposing anyone who was a conscientious objector holding union office. Some farmers were unhappy about employing COs and even where they did, farm workers and land girls often refused to work alongside them; some land girls being more prepared to work with German POWs than with COs, whom they despised as cowards.

Tribunals frequently made life as difficult as possible. In one instance, reported in what was then the *Manchester Guardian*, a conscientious objector made thirty unsuccessful applications for jobs until finally being accepted by a sympathetic firm at a salary of 30s a week, which was half his usual salary. When the chairman of the local tribunal was told, he remarked that the firm, being sympathetic, might offer more money and refused to sanction the work, which meant the CO was forced once again to go looking for work. To quote John Graham, the tribunal had effectively 'punished him as a bad citizen, instead of granting exemption to which he was by law entitled' and he states that the system made possibly considerable instances of 'petty tyrannies'. It did but the tribunal system was operating against the background of a punitive war where thousands were enlisting only to be slaughtered in the trenches; for tribunal members, to say nothing of families up and down the country whose men were fighting, the behaviour of conscientious objectors was incomprehensible and if they were not prepared to kill or be killed for King and country, their lives should at least be made as uncomfortable as possible.

Humanitarian service

From the very beginning of the war, some pacifists and war resisters whose humanitarian or religious beliefs meant they would not take part in killing nevertheless felt they could not stand aside; they wanted to do something to help those who were suffering. The Society of Friends set up two main humanitarian organisations: the Friends Relief Service and what became the FAU. Members of the Friends Relief Service worked with civilians only; the FAU was prepared to work alongside the troops. Both were voluntary civilian organisations but FAU members wore a khaki uniform.

A small group of Quakers launched the FAU in autumn 'to render voluntary non-service in relief of the suffering and distress resulting from war. Members, who did not necessarily have to be Quakers, went to France as early as October 1914. The first group numbered 43 men; by the end of the war membership totalled well over 1,000, with 600 in France. During the course of the war, the FAU set up dozens of hospitals in France; they staffed dressing stations on the front line, provided motor ambulances that moved 260,000 sick and wounded men away from the battlefields, had 4 ambulance trains, which moved ½ million seriously wounded men, and 2 hospital ships that carried 33,000 men back to Britain. In Belgium the FAU inoculated 27,000 Belgians against typhoid, fed and clothed refugees and helped to start lace-making and other industries. The Unit distributed milk and purified water. All members worked as volunteers, without pay. Initially, the FAU worked for the French army but subsequently closely with the British army. They treated not just British casualties but also German. FAU members also worked with the sick and needy in British hospitals.

When conscription came in, members of the FAU got almost automatic exemption, conditional on continuing the humanitarian work they were doing. However, at this point some men left the FAU. They had willingly volunteered to work with the FAU on humanitarian grounds but were not prepared to continue once they were compelled to do so. Instead they returned to Britain to stand with their fellow conscientious objectors, even if it meant prison.

Corder Catchpool was a Quaker. He believed that war was 'contrary to the will of God, as revealed in the life and teaching of Jesus Christ ...' and was therefore 'unable to enlist or bear arms, either for offence or defence'. Soon after the war began he experienced a call to take up ambulance work, believing that 'there might be great opportunities for service … in tending the wounded and dying …'. Accordingly, he joined the newly formed FAU and in October 1914, after training, was one of the first to go to France. Having first helped to rescue the crew of a torpedo ship, he and the rest of the group finally arrived in Dunkirk, where conditions were appalling and the need for medical help was desperate. Large warehouses at the port were being used as temporary stations for the wounded, who were waiting to be shipped to hospitals at Le Havre:

> I shall never in my life forget the sight and sounds that met us. Figure two huge goods sheds, semi-dark, every inch of floor space … covered with the flimsy French stretchers, so that in places you had to step on them to get about – and on each stretcher a wounded man – desperately wounded, nearly every one. The air heavy with the stench of putrid flesh, and thick with groans and cries …

Initially, he worked loading the wounded onto hospital ships to be sent back to Britain, turning away to vomit when the stench was too great. Then he was based at a dressing station at Malo-les-Bains, Dunkirk, moving at regular intervals to makeshift hospitals and clearing stations just behind the front line to treat the wounded there. Corder Catchpool sent regular letters home describing his experiences and the appalling wounds that the FAU were attempting to treat, which were published in 1919 as *On Two Fronts: Letters of a Conscientious Objector*. His writings paint a vivid picture of the horrors of war, life on the front line and his feelings of belief in what he was doing. Like many COs, he respected the fighting men and their principles but believed that all had been duped into war:

> It is grand the way men give all – their comfort, their lives, gladly to serve their country, in a cause they believe to be right. But when I look out of my window … and see the bright starlit sky prostituted by those blood-red patches of flame, I turn away sick at heart … and think that they with all the sublimity of their sacrifice, are dupes; we, dupes; all the world, dupes of the handfuls of charlatans who make wars, exploiting, trading upon, those nobler traits of human nature. 'Your country needs you,' cry armament manufacturer, Junker, Chauvenist, well knowing that at that cry millions of hearts that beat

true and honest will begin to beat proudly and courageously, and millions of men will march out to slay their brothers.

As the war continued, Catchpool, who became one of the FAU's leading members, was horrified that it had gone on for so long with such wastage of life. He also came to believe that the war was being organised like a 'huge business'. He was sure that his decision to try and help the suffering had been the right one, even though sometimes there was little they could do other than provide some comfort. In January 1916 he was at home on leave in Britain as the Quaker yearly meeting was discussing the forthcoming introduction of conscription and reaffirming total opposition to compulsory military service. Catchpool returned to France but by now thought that the FAU was working too closely with the army. In May 1916 he left the Unit, believing that it had become 'in effect a conscript unit'.

When conscription had been introduced, FAU members were almost automatically given exemption conditional on continuing their work with the FAU but Catchpool was not prepared to do this. His service had been voluntary not compulsory. He appeared before his local and an appeal tribunal, applying for absolute exemption on pacifist grounds and refused to take alternative service under the Act, 'for this would imply a bargain with militarism, which I believe to be utterly wrong.' He was arrested in January 1917 and subsequently court-martialled and imprisoned. After he was released from prison in 1919, he worked with the Friends War Victims Relief Committee in Berlin, helping the victims of war and reparation.

Another who joined the FAU and left for the same reasons was Richard Porteous. Born in 1896, he was 18 when the war began. He belonged to the Presbyterian Church and was a member of the Christian pacifist group, the FoR. He also joined the N-CF. For Porteous, all war was 'contrary to the spirit of love by which Christ lived'.

By 1915 Porteous was working with the Unit in Malo, near Dunkirk, where the FAU had a central ambulance depot. He was based at the Hotel du Kursaal, which was run by the FAU as a hospital and helped to treat casualties from the second Battle of Ypres in April and May 1915. He left the Unit in 1916 when conscription was introduced and returned to Britain. According to his niece, Felicia Shanahan, who found a report on his time in the FAU in the Society of Friends Library in London, 'It was truly touching to see his report: "Very capable and highly efficient in all kinds of work".'

Aged 21 Porteous appeared before his local tribunal in Camberwell in September 1916. When asked what he was doing at the time, he replied that he had 'recently been tramping through the country distributing literature [FoR and other pacifist literature] to folk on the road, entering into conversation wherever possible and interviewing ministers of all denominations in the places I have passed through'. He was also asked whether he had left the FAU because 'he was of military age' to which he replied:

> No, Sir, as a member of the Unit I was presented by the War Office with a certificate of absolute exemption on conscientious grounds. On my return home I entered into a long correspondence with Sir George Newman, the Chairman of the Unit, respecting this certificate, but when I finally refused to remain a member of the Unit … he returned the certificate to the War Office and they cancelled it immediately.

The clerk of the tribunal then asked Porteous why he had left the Unit and Porteous replied:

> It is not an easy matter to explain. After the passing of the Military Service Act the voluntary nature of the unit largely disappeared … a number of us drew up a memorial, which was to have been presented to the Government expressing our motive in undertaking work out there & giving expression to our sympathy with the conscientious objectors at home …

The other reason that he gave was that he 'felt a positive call to greater service over here, that is work for peace'. Porteous' tribunal questioning followed much the same pattern as questioning in all tribunals, with the tribunal members clearly having considerable difficulty in understanding his position and his deeply held belief that his pacifism and religious beliefs superseded the demands of the State. Not surprisingly, the tribunal, who cut his father's testimony short, directed him into non-combatant duties in the army. He was called up on 8 January 1917 but refused to present himself to the army unit. He was arrested five days later and taken to Streethouse police station in Birmingham and placed in the cells. From there he was taken to Norton

Barracks, Worcester, where he refused orders, was court-martialled and imprisoned in Wormwood Scrubs. He served a second prison sentence in Dorchester.

A difficult and thankless task

While several thousand conscientious objectors accepted alternative civilian service, and even non-combatant duties, absolutists refused to do so. Their decision was completely incomprehensible to tribunals, the public and the right-wing press. An editorial in *The Times*, dated 8 April 1916, which followed the Bishop of Lincoln's letter some days earlier, launched a swingeing attack on conscientious objectors who refused alternative service:

> Objection to taking life may be and is allowed as a valid plea; but objection to ambulance or hospital work or to digging trenches justly exposes the holder to contempt. He is endeavouring to escape the obligations he owes to society in return for the protection which he claims and enjoys. He is a parasite and deserves to be treated as a pariah.

Clifford Allen had outlined the reasons for his refusal in his piece in the *Tribunal*. Richard Porteous described his reasons in a letter dated 26 September 1916, following the decision of his local tribunal to exempt him from combatant service only. Having acknowledged the decision, he wrote:

> It may have appeared unreasonable that I should refuse to undertake some useful civil labour but I am very sure that if the members of the Tribunal were young men, being as they are heart & soul in the war, they would not be content with farming or anything else but would want to be in the fight. Now I believe in peace with all my being; I believe in it for the sake of the men of all the nations in the trenches who are being maimbed [*sic*] & slaughtered every day; I believe in it for the mothers & the little children & I believe that the time has come to work for it & that is why I am not content to grow cabbages. I much appreciate the courteous hearing which I received, & although I must regard their decision, after I had made it plain to them that I could not possibly accept non-combatant service, as a very stupid one. I wish them well in their difficult & thankless task.

Chapter 5

Handed Over to the Army

'*I was a Conscientious Objector and wouldn't be a soldier*'
Fred Murfin

Around 8,000 conscientious objectors found themselves in the army for one or more periods of time. There were 2,500 conscientious objectors who had their applications for exemption turned down completely and were sent into combatant units. About 1,200 refused to attend tribunals; most were tracked down and again placed in combatant units. In addition, tribunals directed about 5,000 objectors into non-combatant service, some 3,400 being enlisted in the NCC.

Put into the army unwillingly, thousands of conscientious objectors refused to accept military discipline, something that Asquith and his Cabinet had not really expected. They had probably assumed that once tribunals had made their decisions, objectors would accept their lot and go quietly. After all, under the Military Service Act, any eligible man who had not been exempted was 'deemed' to have been enlisted and was therefore already a soldier – in the eyes of the law. For conscientious objectors however this was not the case: whether placed in combatant or non-combatant units most refused to accept military status and orders. They saw themselves as civilians and were not prepared to accept the military: it would have completely contradicted their beliefs. As a result, commanding officers up and down the country were frequently baffled and confused by courteous but determined men who stood in front of them refusing to accept military discipline.

The consequences of resistance could be and frequently were dire: while in some units commanding officers attempted to persuade conscientious objectors to accept the military, in others army officers used extreme brutality and intimidation to try and get objectors to become soldiers. What surprised both army and government was just how far COs would take their resistance. Before conscription had been in place for more than three or four months, it became clear that COs were even prepared to die for their principles.

Being handed over

Any CO who did not receive absolute exemption or exemption conditional on doing civilian work would in due course receive call-up papers. Some COs accepted call-up and went into a unit, reserving their resistance until such time as they were actually in the unit. Most ignored their call-up papers when they arrived. In due course they were arrested, fined and handed over to the army.

Mark Hayler was a Quaker and came from a long line of activists, his paternal grandfather having been a Chartist. When war began he was working with young boys in a reform school in Liverpool and he wrote to Lord Derby explaining that he could not be counted on to fight. He later used the letter as evidence at his tribunal. Hayler considered going into the Red Cross or the RAMC but felt that he would only be 'patching people up' to send them back to fight, something he was not prepared to do. He linked up with other pacifists and they thought about hiding away in Scotland but in the event the plans did not materialise and he appeared before a tribunal in Liverpool, which refused him exemption. When he returned to the school, his employer asked him not to be arrested on the school premises, as so many of the boys had been through the police courts.

Hayler cycled to his parents' house in London, where the police came to arrest him on Good Friday. He was working on a map of the world for Arthur Mee's *Children's Encyclopedia*: 'I hadn't quite finished. I noticed a policeman coming up the path … My feeling was that I mustn't put the policeman in a difficult position. He had his job to do. I said to him, "Let me finish this map and I'll come down to the station." But he had orders to arrest me. I went down to the station with him.' He stayed in a police cell overnight where he said they were 'very decent' and next morning was taken to Croydon town hall, which to his astonishment was packed with fifty or sixty supporters, most of them Quakers. Following his case, he was escorted to Kingston Barracks, where he was put in the guardroom. At that point he was the only CO in the guardroom, though others began arriving soon afterwards.

Interviewed by the IWM in 1974, Hayler described how no one knew what to do with them: 'It was disturbing for the sergeant because we claimed we were civilians. It was too new, it had never happened before; they didn't tumble to it for some weeks … We were a nuisance.' He refused to obey orders, was court-martialled and sent to Wandsworth where he served his first prison term. Following his release, he was sent back to barracks, where despite being bullied, he refused orders and was kept isolated in a tent, guarded by two soldiers, being fed scrapings from other meals. At his court martial he said: 'For refusing to be a soldier I am told I may have to forfeit my life … I thought the days of religious persecution were over and that an Englishman could hold and express his convictions.'

Non-Combatant Corps

In March 1916 the NCC was set up as a special unit within the army. Dubbed the No-Courage Corps by the popular press, the unit was, as its name suggests, a non-combatant unit and according to a statement from the War Office, reported in *The Times* of 13 March 1916, was formed 'for conscientious objectors'. Apart from the officers, who were from the regular army, most of the men in the NCC were COs, who were given the rank of army privates. They were subject to army rules and discipline, which involved saluting, drilling and wearing a khaki uniform but were not expected to handle weapons or engage in fighting, According to the War Office, they were to be employed on 'the repair of roads and railways, sanitation, the provision of huts and baths for soldiers coming out of the trenches, and the manufacture and provision of many necessaries of life'. According to *The Times*, the formation of the NCC, which they described as the 'pick and shovel brigade', was greeted with relief by men already serving in other non-combatant units, namely the Royal Medical Army Corps (RAMC), who were not anxious to welcome conscientious objectors as comrades.

The government and tribunals saw the NCC as the obvious solution for men who for reasons of conscience were not prepared to engage in killing. They would not have to fight but they could do useful work in the military. According to a statement by Mr Harold Tennant, Under Secretary for War, putting COs in the NCC might also release men from non-combatant duties who would fight. The N-CF opposed the NCC from the very start, saying in the *Tribunal* that Tennant's statement 'bears out the contention that by undertaking non-combatant service a conscientious objector would therefore be assisting in the prosecution of the war and directly releasing others to do that which he feels it is not right for him to perform himself'. The N-CF's opposition to the NCC also extended to the RAMC, which they considered also to be part of 'the military machine, its primary function being to maintain the efficiency of the fighting forces, and re-equip the wounded for further fighting', a view that the RAMC vehemently rejected. Either way, the N-CF stated that 'the Government should understand that the men for whom we speak, can, under no circumstances, become part of this corps, which we observe will be under the control of the War Office and in every sense part of the military machine'.

How far a conscientious objector took his stand was always an individual decision. Some COs who were profoundly opposed to killing were prepared to carry out non-combatant duties and said so when applying for exemption. Alfred Evans was a conscientious objector but on humanitarian grounds was willing to serve in the RAMC and was granted exemption from combat service, conditional on doing so. However, things did not turn out as he had hoped. On 25 April 1916 he reported to a recruiting office in Ealing Broadway but when he presented his certificate of exemption to a lieutenant, it was torn up and he was told that he was to be enlisted in the NCC. Evans refused to sign the official paper, the guard was called and he was taken under military escort to Hounslow Barracks. Subsequently, he was sent to Harwich Redoubt.

Horace Eaton thought long and hard about how far to take his objection. When the war began, 'the question often occurred to my mind as to whether I could not do something for the wounded and suffering. So I took up a course of training in the St John's Ambulance and attempted to join the RAMC through the recruiting office at Bradford, but without success – seeing I had not passed an examination.' Eaton's tribunal gave him exemption from combatant duties; he asked to be allowed to join the FAU but this was turned down:

A non-combatant corps had been formed by the military authorities for conscientious objectors. It was understood at first their duties would be to bury the dead on the battlefields and other unpleasant tasks in the trenches. So here was another big problem! Should I refuse all service to the country in which I had been brought up and thus be sent to prison – or should I undertake non-combatant duties! For over a fortnight I pondered over the matter but could not definitely decide which was the right path … Much of my time was spent outdoors as I was liable to arrest any day as an absentee. I seemed to be led to the conclusion that the right way was to undertake any service I could conscientiously perform, which would not take life or assist to take the life of another. So accordingly I called at the Bradford Recruiting Office on Friday June 16, 1916.

Eaton spent his first night away in a 'tram-shed called a barracks'. He tried to sleep on the rough blankets and bed boards provided – a massive change from his own comfortable bed – and noticed that the barracks were full of young men, whom he said looked as if 'they had been released from some chains – whereas if they had only realised it they had entered into a kind of slavery'.

After a medical examination and trying on his uniform, Eaton with the rest of his unit was sent to Richmond Castle, North Yorkshire, which served as an NCC base. John Brocklesby was also posted there. At Richmond Castle, COs worked alongside regular soldiers, building stables for army horses, preparing fields for landing strips, moving supplies and organising accommodation for soldiers. Other NCC units were sent to camps elsewhere in England and France. The work was hard and there were times when it clashed with COs' principles. As Eaton described: 'One day a part of our company were sent to the railway station to unload a railway van for another company of soldiers. They moved almost everything except some rifles and ammunition and these they refused to handle. Regular soldiers had to be called upon to finish the work.' A similar situation occurred with an NCC unit in Newhaven. The men refused to load munitions and were, as a result, court-martialled and thirty-eight men were sentenced to six months imprisonment with hard labour. Describing this situation, Eaton commented: 'This for obeying conscience! Oh Christian (?) England, the home of the free?'

Being in non-combatant units also meant COs were witness to sights that confirmed their anti-war principles. Eaton and Fred Murfin both commented on seeing soldiers undertaking bayonet practice and throwing mock bombs. For Eaton, 'the practice of bayonet fighting alone is utterly detestable and disgusting. The young fellows I have seen being trained in this way – or most of them – were evidently shocked or sickened ... They had generally to be cursed or bullied into it ...'. Murfin, who was sent into a non-combatant unit at Seaford, wrote in his account that 'I heard of one young man who couldn't do this bayonet practice – he was vomiting so badly ... everyone should see this disgusting practice'.

Resistance

Some COs were prepared to accept non-combatant service but there were many others who were not: they objected to all forms of military service, whether combatant or non-combatant and were determined to resist. Similarly, COs were also resisting in combatants units. Resistance meant disobeying orders and punishments were severe.

On arrival newcomers had to sign documents for pay and equipment, put on a uniform or go for a medical examination. For Howard Marten, resistance over dress was undignified:

> After I had been rejected by the tribunals, I was committed to a magistrate's court to await a military escort ... I was handed over to a military escort and taken to Mill Hill Barracks. Then the first thing you had to face was putting on a uniform ... you either had to accept uniform and take it or you had to sit on or lay on the floor and kick. Well, I wasn't prepared to do undignified things. I said to the NCOs in charge, 'Look here. I suppose you've got orders to dress me forcibly. I have no objection to putting on a uniform but it won't alter my attitude'. And I compromised in that way.

Fred Murfin's first tribunal directed him into non-combatant service and he took his case to appeal. At the appeal tribunal, the military representative asked him if he would kill wild beasts, to which Murfin replied: 'The Germans are not wild beasts, sir!' Once again non-combatant orders were confirmed and Murfin waited to be arrested. On 21 May 1916 his landlord told him that the police had come to his lodgings. The police returned and gave him a few days to present himself at the police station. He returned to work, wrote to his parents to tell them what was happening, and said goodbye to Quaker friends, who promised to support him. On 25 May he reported to the police station and was put into an unlocked cell. That evening other COs were brought into the cells, including Stuart Beavis and Alfred Taylor. Beavis and Murfin were to spend the next three years together in prison.

Murfin and the others appeared at the magistrate court, where they were charged as 'deserters from the army' and were fined. Refusing to pay, the men were taken under military escort to Mill Hill Recruiting Station, where they were told to strip for a medical examination. Failure to do so would result in their clothes being torn off them. Murfin did strip but 'was as unhelpful as I knew how to be. I kept my feet on the ground when weighed, told the eye doctor I couldn't help him and the heart doctor the same thing, telling each that I was a Conscientious Objector and wouldn't be a soldier.' Soon afterwards they were taken to the stores to be given their uniforms:

> Kit bags were put round our necks. I refused to give the size of anything and the men had to guess … All the things were piled into the bag … As I wouldn't carry the thing, the bag was hung round my neck; then one man on either side and one behind ran me to the another department, pressing on the bag and nearly strangling me.

Apparently, Murfin's throat still hurt nearly forty-five years later. Next came the putting on of the uniform: 'The officer said, "Now my lads, we want you to put khaki on." We all refused, I think, and we each had a soldier to undress and dress us. My attendant suggested that, as my feet smelled so badly, I'd better see to my own socks! I did, and we both enjoyed the joke.' Murfin thought that the soldier was a 'nice fellow' and commented that, as a rule, if officers were decent, so too were the men, something that other COs would have agreed with.

From Mill Hill Murfin and the other COs were taken by train to Seaford Camp, where they were met by an officer who told them they had very few problems with non-combatant men and that if they fell in with the rest, they would start with a clean sheet, to which Murfin and the others replied: 'We will refuse to obey all military orders on conscientious grounds'.

Brutal punishments
COs who refused military orders were frequently bullied, intimidated, forcibly dressed, beaten and brutalised as the army attempted to break their resistance. Eventually, refusal to obey orders led to court martial and a prison sentence.

George Dutch was a Quaker and a socialist. In 1915 he set up a Tunbridge branch of the N-CF. After serving one prison sentence, he was posted to Maxton Camp, near Dover:

> The major was very unpleasant, hectoring. 'Well,' he said when he'd read my statement, 'all I can say is that in my opinion conscientious objection is just another name for cowardice' – very insulting and unpleasant … Then he said, 'Take him away! Take him away and don't put a rag on him, he's got to dress himself [in army uniform].' And of course the NCOs did as they were told. I was taken back, and they stripped me of my own clothing and put the uniform down beside me and said, 'Now you've got to put it on.' I said, 'I will not put it on.' They said, 'All right, you've got to sit there.' I sat there.

After a day or two the tent that Dutch was in was taken up and put right on top of the cliff overlooking the sea:

> This was in November and it was pretty cold, misty weather. My uniform was put beside me again by the tent pole, and, just to make things worse than ever, they rolled the tent walls up so that the wind came right into the tent … and I could just sit there and freeze, which I did. The orders were that no one was to come near me until I dressed and came down. Well I didn't dress and didn't go down. I stayed there … I think it must have been at least ten days – and nights – in just my singlet and pants … I was frozen right through with exposure. So frozen that I didn't feel a lot, I was just insensitive, I just sat there and set my teeth to stick whatever came.

Interestingly, Dutch's first encounter at Maxton had been with an elderly colonel who was very friendly and said he felt he could not send Dutch back to prison again. He had tried to persuade Dutch to enter a non-combatant battalion and said he would personally try and find him some work that was not fighting. On Dutch refusing the offer, the colonel, not knowing what to do with him, sent him home. Dutch was subsequently arrested and on return to Maxton found himself in front of the 'hectoring' major, who was highly unpopular with the soldiers.

Another CO, Horace Twilley, who refused all military orders was first placed on remand, then sentenced to twenty-eight days' field punishment, which he was told by a sergeant would break his spirit. Twilley refused orderly duties, which were part of the punishment and was placed in irons for 2 hours. The following morning he was:

> fetched out forcibly and rushed to the parade ground. Hauled around for an hour by one soldier after another, until exhausted – scores of soldiers laughing at me. Afternoon, again dragged out of room and dragged with other conscientious objectors round the parade ground. One burley Sergeant caught me by collar and in the small of the back and propelled me thus for about a hundred yards … I was put in irons for two hours, and am told this will be done every one of the 28 days 'to tame me' …

'They can have my body, my mind I will destroy rather than allow the military cult to take it. I was flooded for weeks in my cell with water, two buckets of creosol were thrown in, and I was gassed. I was naked for several days and nights in chains.'

J.B. Saunders, sentenced to hard labour and punished for refusing orders, Alexandria, Egypt; account printed in the *Tribunal*, 20 September 1917

Despite the brutality, COs continued to resist. Punishments became so harsh they could best be described as torture. At Harwich Redoubt, a fortress that had been built to house French prisoners during the Napoleonic Wars, COs who refused orders were strapped into straitjackets, and made to stand in hot sun for hours on end. Others, such as Harry Stanton, were placed in punishment cells, overrun with rats and kept on bread and water or even no food at all. There were three cells, built into a hill; the only light that reached the second cell came from a filthy window. The cells were freezing cold; floorboards were rotten and moisture trickled down the walls. Harry Stanton was placed in the second cell; by standing on tiptoe under the window, he was able to read for a short time each day. He was kept without food for three days.

There were many instances of barbaric cruelty meted out to conscientious objectors 'deemed' to be soldiers in the army. One, which was highlighted in the press, concerned a conscientious objector called

James Brightmore, a solicitor's clerk from Manchester. Refused exemption, he was imprisoned for eight months then in June 1917 was posted to an army unit in Cleethorpes. There he was sentenced to twenty-eight days' solitary confinement in an uncovered pit 3ft wide at its top and about 10–12ft deep. At its bottom the pit was so full of water that Brightmore had to stand on two strips of wood just above the water line. In a letter home, that he said might be his last, he wrote: 'There is no room to walk about, and sitting is impossible. The sun beats down and through the long day there are only the walls of clay to look at. Already I am half mad.' A friendly soldier smuggled his letter out of the camp and described how all Brightmore had in the pit was a blanket or two and an oil sheet for cover. Constantly sworn at and abused, it was useless for Brightmore to complain because orders had been given that no one should listen to him. To add to his torture, Brightmore was told, and believed, that five of his friends had been taken to France and shot and that he too would be sent to France with the next draft. An account of Brightmore's treatment was published in the *Manchester Guardian* on 30 June 1917. Soon after, Brightmore was taken out of the pit, which was filled in and attempts were made to conceal the incident. Subsequently, the major responsible was dismissed.

Another case was that of a conscientious objector named Jack Gray at Hornsea Camp. Gray had already served a prison term and following this was sent back into the army – the so-called 'cat and mouse treatment' whereby COs were court-martialled, imprisoned, released, court-martialled, imprisoned and so on. Refusing to salute an officer, a live Mills bomb was thrown at his feet. Bravely, Gray refused to throw the bomb when ordered to do so. Continuing to disobey all military orders, Gray was beaten and sworn at by the company major, who ordered him to carry a pack filled with stones on a forced march. He was also stripped naked, had a rope tied around his abdomen and was then thrown into a filthy pond eight or nine times, each time being dragged out by the rope. Apparently the squad who were told to 'break him in' finally refused to continue torturing him but Gray, by now completely broken, abandoned his resistance.

Many individual COs recorded the treatment they experienced; others such as Quaker John Graham noted instances they heard about, either from letters, scribbled notes or word or mouth so that today the evidence of brutality towards COs in the army is well documented.

Horace Eaton, in Richmond Castle, made careful notes of incidences of brutality that he observed, later compiling those and his own story into his memoirs. Writing about the abuse at Richmond Castle, he said: 'I had not quite the attitude as these young fellows, yet I admired their courageous stand, and attitude towards the bullying methods of militarism. The methods adopted to try and make these young fellows into non-combatants or soldiers often made one's blood boil with indignation …' In his writings he notes that one young CO, S. Cooper of Leeds, had actually gone insane because of the treatment he received. In fact, thirty-one COs eventually went insane because of brutality either in the army or prison. Compared with the thousands who died and suffered in the trenches, the number may seem insignificant but COs who went insane did so because they were brutalised simply because they refused to kill. As Horace Eaton commented: 'We hear talk of Prussian militarism and all its inhuman treatment – but it appeared to me that all militarism was pretty much the same.'

Sentenced to death
In May and June 1916 the army took punishment and intimidation to an even more extreme level when it sent a number of conscientious objectors over to France and sentenced them to death. The aim was both to make an example of them and to intimidate others into submission. As Quaker, journalist and CO Hubert Peet described it, this 'marked the crest of the wave in the efforts of the military authorities to break the [CO] movement'. The whole operation was carried out in secret, probably without the knowledge of the government, and had it not been for quick thinking, which enabled information to reach the N-CF, the men might have been shot.

In all fifty conscientious objectors, most of them in punishment cells for refusing military orders, were taken to France from Britain. They were sent in three separate groups. The first to go were seventeen COs from the Harwich Redoubt. They included Alfred Evans and Harry Stanton, who had been placed in the freezing, damp and dark cells. According to Stanton's account, on Saturday 6 May he and others were taken before a Colonel Croft:

> it was clear from the faces of the men who preceded me that something serious had happened. When my turn came I found the

Colonel surrounded by a large group of officers of lesser rank. 'I am sorry to tell you,' he said slowly, 'that I am instructed by the War Office to cancel the order for your district court martial, and to send you to France with the 2nd Company of the Eastern Non-Combatant Corps.' The news came as a shock, though the decision was not entirely unexpected. Our guards had repeatedly told us that we should 'soon be pushing the daisies up'.

The men were told they would be taken in irons to France where they would be put under 'active service conditions' and if they continued to resist military orders would be shot. They were told to take their pay and make their wills; all seventeen COs refused. The men were then moved from Harwich during the night, taken across London and then to Southampton where a boat was waiting.

At much the same time another group of sixteen conscientious objectors from Richmond Castle in Yorkshire were also being moved. One of them was John Brocklesby.

Following an appeal tribunal, Brocklesby had been directed into non-combatant service. He and one of his two brothers were playing billiards when the police arrived to arrest him. His father persuaded the police to leave him overnight and the next morning he walked into Conisborough police station. He appeared at Doncaster magistrate court and was remanded in custody to await a military escort. He spent most of the day in a cell – a Mrs Holland, caretaker of the Doncaster Friends Meeting House, sent in some food – and was then taken by military escort to Pontefract Barracks and placed in the guardroom. For Brocklesby his first night 'in the army' was the most uncomfortable night of his life. There were thirty men in a room designed for fifteen, with five broad-hinged shelves on the wall that provided a sleeping space for three men. Those who could not get a shelf slept on the floor. The stench of humanity and drunks combined with the 'crowning stench of a filthy latrine in the corner of which the drain was choked and urine was seeping across the floor'. Bert knew that his sufferings were as nothing compared to the sufferings of millions caused by 'this cursed war' but, coming from a comfortable home, the experience was a shock. The following day he was sent to join the NCC unit at Richmond Castle, where he immediately began to refuse orders and was sentenced to three days' solitary confinement on bread and water. A hole in his cell wall enabled him to communicate and play a game of chess with a fellow CO, Norman Gaudie. A few days later, he and the other COs were on their way to France.

An amusing incident

John Brocklesby was a big man, something that caused an 'amusing incident' when he was at Richmond Castle:

the captain decided that all the resisters should do drill. I determined to be strictly passive. We were put in our places along with the other NCC men and Sergeant Foster was allotted to make me do the drill. The captain himself gave the orders. For the arm exercises Foster shot my arms in and out. When we came to 'double knee bend' the squad sank earthward and left us prominently erect. The captain shouted to Foster, 'If he won't go down, shove him down.' Quite unresisting down I went and lay passively on the floor, thinking to myself, 'They shoved me down, they can hoist me up also.' As the squad rose, Foster hoisted me up by the pants. Then he gasped, 'I'll have a go at one of those little chaps,' and left. The captain soon decided it was useless and had us marched back to our cells feeling we had won that hurdle.

According to Brocklesby, when the information came through that they were to be moved to France, eight of the group were in the guardroom, eight were in the cells. When the guard came to turn the men out from the guardroom, the COs resisted, clinging to chairs, tables and doorframes. As a result they were badly manhandled. Brocklesby went to see the captain and said he would sort it out:

I said, 'Look here, chaps, it's no good offering resistance to these orders. If you use force to resist, I can tell you the Army knows all about force and you don't stand any chance. We must rely on spiritual force. For my part, they can take me where they will, even into the front line trenches, but they will never get me to raise my hand against my fellow man.'

The COs stopped resisting and were taken to Southampton, where they were joined by a third group of COs from Seaford Camp.

According to Brocklesby, the men from Seaford 'carried marks of rough treatment'.

Fred Murfin was one of the Seaford group. While at Seaford, evidence had been taken for Murfin's court martial and in his account 'Prisoners for Peace', he mentions that the lieutenant who took his particulars only had one arm:

> He was very abusive and told me that he had lost his arm defending me. I replied: 'You lost your arm whilst you were trying to destroy someone else.' This made him mad. He kept calling me Private Murfin. I said I wasn't a Private. He said I was. We repeated this a few times, then I said: 'You may think I am but I am not a private. I am a prisoner'.

A day later an officer came to tell Murfin and the others that they were being sent to France and would they go willingly or in handcuffs. They refused; their hands were handcuffed behind their backs and they were marched to the station. One of their number, Stuart Beavis refused to walk, sat down and was manhandled to his feet, his glasses being broken in the process. Eventually, they too arrived at Southampton. Asking to see the officer in command before they boarded the ship, they repeated their protest, stating that they were religious objectors to all warfare and 'we shall refuse to obey all military orders and shall only move under escort. We are prisoners, not soldiers.'

None of the COs was given the opportunity to inform friends and family that they were being shipped out to France. Happily, however, somebody on the train, which was taking the Harwich group across London, managed to write and throw a note out of the train, telling whoever read it that COs were being taken to France. With this information the N-CF and Quaker groups swung into action. On 9 May Professor Gilbert Murray, regis professor of Greek at Oxford University, who advocated a more humane treatment of conscientious objectors, dashed to the House of Commons and managed to see Lord Derby, who confirmed that the objectors would be shot. According to his own account, Murray managed to see Asquith, who was apparently appalled by the situation and immediately sent a telegram to the Commander-in-Chief saying that no death sentences were to be carried out without Cabinet approval.

By the time the N-CF knew what was happening, the Harwich group had arrived at what was known as Cinder City Camp in Le Havre.

Knowing that the consequence of refusing orders would be severe, they nevertheless started resistance and what Hubert Peet describes as 'an extraordinary scene' took place. They were sent out onto a vast parade ground containing about 1,000 soldiers lined up before 30 officers. The COs were bundled into their places in various groups and the parade was then ordered to 'shun, right turn, quick march'. Not a single conscientious objector moved. According to Alfred Evans:

> There was a lot of shouting, movement among the officers and the NCOs as the mass of the men nearly reached the edge of the parade ground and small parties were sent back and we were dragged off. But for a short time it must have been an amazing sight to see this small group of us scattered motionless over the huge parade ground.

Hubert Peet writing about the event commented proudly that 'dotted around the parade ground were 17 conscientious objectors still in their original positions. And in their original positions in every sense they stood to the end, the bulwark of the movement, tested and not found wanting.'

Over the next few days, the objectors were beaten, bullied and manhandled. The army used every method to try and break their resistance, threatening the death sentence and even, Brocklesby remembered, telling some of the COs who arrived after the Harwich group that their comrades had already been shot. As the situation intensified, some of the Harwich group were moved to a Field Punishment Unit at Harfleur and given twenty-eight days' field punishment.

Field Punishment No. 1 was the most brutal punishment in the army. It involved strapping a man with chains, ropes or leather straps to a rigid object such as a post, wheel or fence, and stretching out his arms in the shape of a crucifix. Tied tightly, the man was unable to move and was left in this position for 2 hours, daily for three days. Following a break the sequence began again for another three days until the twenty-eight days had been completed. The punishment was legal and was applied to ordinary soldiers not just COs. Harry Stanton, who kept a detailed diary, described his first experience of the punishment:

> We were placed with our backs to the posts and arms outstretched. Our ankles were then tied together and our arms tied tightly at the

wrists to the cross-beams. We were to remain in this position for two hours. For those of us who were of average height the strain upon our arms were just bearable, though our wrists quickly became numbed, but for those who were shorter, the punishment was painful in the extreme, since they were forced to stand entirely on their toes to relieve their arms of the dead weight of the body.

The following evening, the same punishment took place but with a difference – this time the men were tied to barbed wire:

We were placed with our faces to the barbed wire of the inner fence. As the ropes with which we were tied fastened round the barbed wire instead of the usual thick posts, it was possible to tie them much more tightly, and I found myself drawn so closely to the fence that when I wished to turn my head I had to do so very cautiously to avoid my face being torn by the barbs.

Despite the brutality, COs felt they 'had no special cause to complain that we … were treated in this way – we were exceptional cases, and militarism was making a special effort to break us in. The shamefulness of the system lies in the fact that the ordinary soldier is liable to such punishment for the merest trivial offence.'

From Harfleur the group were taken to Henriville Camp, outside Boulogne; from there they were told they would be taken to the front line and shot. According to Harry Stanton, the soldier who told him this was highly indignant, saying that he would rather shoot the officer who gave the order than shoot the resisters. He told Stanton that he came out to France to shoot Germans, not to murder Englishmen.

It might seem strange but many COs encountered kindness from ordinary soldiers. On one occasion, a soldier sent his dinner to Alfred Evans with his compliments. Alfred Evans never discovered the identity of his benefactor but hoped he had survived the war. A captain of the Irish Guards added his own money to the COs' meagre funds so they could buy food from the canteen and there were other instances where the courage and determination of the COs clearly won the respect of some of the regular army.

Punishment continued at Boulogne as the seventeen Harwich resisters were handcuffed and placed in a dark underground wooden cage, about 12ft square. There was one latrine bucket for seventeen

Fenner Brockway was not among the men who were sent to France but he says that he rarely encountered ill-will from soldiers: 'The soldiers, particularly those who had been to the front, sympathised and often regarded us as "bloody heroes" for defying the "brass hats" ... On our side, we never regarded the soldiers as enemies. We regarded them as victims of Conscription and War, no less than ourselves – indeed, much more than ourselves.'

men, who had to help each other to pull down trousers when they needed to use it. Their rations were restricted to four hard biscuits and 8oz of bully beef a day with heavily chlorinated water to drink. Despite this treatment, the resisters continued their protests, according to Howard Marten remaining determined but civil.

By now the other groups had arrived and managed to get news of their whereabouts back to Britain. To do so, Brocklesby used a field postcard issued to ordinary soldiers, on which were printed standard sentences:

Two of these, which I well remember, might have been specially designed for my needs.

(a) I am being sent to base.
(b) I have not heard from you for a long time.

I crossed off the last three letters of 'base' and everything in the second line but the second and third letters of 'you' and the word 'long'. I made my cancellings look as haphazard as possible but thought it looked blatantly clear. Yet it evaded the overworked censor and told the folk at home: 'I am being sent to b ... ou ... long'

By now questions were being asked about the men in the House of Commons and information was being passed to influential people. A deputation of Free Church ministers obtained a meeting with Lord Kitchener and the Joint Advisory Council sent Hubert Peet and Dr F.B. Meyer to France, with the approval of the War Office.

John ('Bert') Brocklesby. 'I am prepared to die for my principles.' With thanks to Mary Brocklesby for permission.

Manifesto issued by the No-Conscription Fellowship (N-CF), September 1915.

John Brocklesby in the pulpit of the Methodist church, Conisborough, January 1915. His anti-war views angered many in his congregation. With thanks to Mary Brocklesby for permission.

No-Conscription Fellowship committee meeting, 1916. Present were: *Front row, left to right*: C.H. Norman, Dr Alfred Salter, Aylmer Rose, Fenner Brockway, Clifford Allen, Edward Grubb, Will Chamberlain, Catherine Marshall. *Standing, left to right*: Revd Leyton Richards, Morgan Jones, John P. Fletcher, A. Barratt Brown, and Bertrand Russell. With thanks to the Peace Pledge Union.

No-Conscription Fellowship committee members outside Mansion House, 17 May 1916. The N-CF leadership was prosecuted for publishing an article, 'Repeal the Act'. They were fined a total of £800. They refused to pay their fines and five went to prison. *Left to right*: Walter Ayles, J.P.F. Fletcher, Will Chamberlain, A. Barratt Brown, Clifford Allen, Fenner Brockway.

David Thomas, socialist and staunchly anti-war, well known in North Wales for his anti-conscription and anti-war views. With thanks to Angharad Tomos for permission.

Richard Porteous, 'I believe in peace with all my being'. He served with the Friends Ambulance Unit (FAU) in 1915 but left the FAU when conscription was introduced in 1916. He was prepared to volunteer but not to be compelled. With thanks to Felicia Shanahan.

'What a C.O. Feels Like': cartoon produced by G. Micklewright, a conscientious objector, which appeared in a Home Office Work Camp newsletter, 1917. Cyril Heasman's album, with thanks to Naomi Rumball.

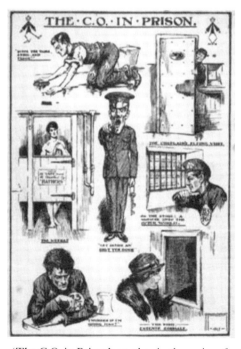

'The C.O. in Prison': another in the series of cartoons produced by Micklewright, showing prison scenes through the eyes of a conscientious objector.

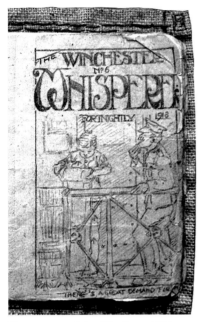

Conscientious objectors at Dyce Work Camp, where conditions were appalling. Many of the men seen here had been sent to France and sentenced to death, commuted to ten years' hard labour. Several of them, including John Brocklesby (second from left, front row), left the Home Office Scheme and returned to prison as absolutists. With thanks to the Peace Pledge Union.

Front cover of the *Winchester Whisperer*, one of the tiny newspapers that conscientious objectors produced in prison, right under the noses of the warders. With thanks to the Peace Pledge Union.

Line drawings of prison life produced by Henry Sargent, later curator of Bexhill Museum. Sargent took the Home Office Scheme and was sent to Princetown Work Centre, formerly Dartmoor Prison. His drawings include images of the prison 'uniform' and the inside of his cell. Cell doors were kept unlocked at Princetown and COs on the scheme were allowed more possessions than absolutists in prisons such as Wormwood Scrubs and Maidstone. From the Sargent Collection, Bexhill Musem, with thanks to Margaret Sargent.

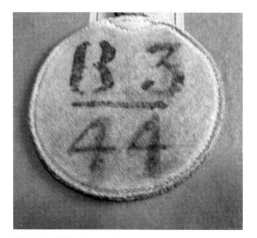

Felt identification badge belonging to Cyril Heasman. The badge was worn on prison clothes and showed the CO's cell number. Thanks to Naomi Rumball.

As this news cutting reports, Cyril Heasman, like many COs, refused to obey his tribunal decision and simply ignored the summons to join the army. He was fined, escorted to the army, refused orders and was court-martialled. Thanks to Naomi Rumball.

Cyril Heasman, engraver and conscientious objector. Heasman accepted the Home Office Scheme and was sent to Princetown Work Camp. Thanks to Naomi Rumball.

Cell door, Princetown Work Camp. Cyril Heasman's album, with thanks to Naomi Rumball.

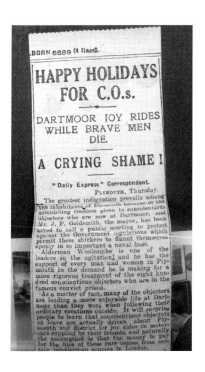

HAPPY HOLIDAYS FOR C.O.s.

DARTMOOR JOY RIDES WHILE BRAVE MEN DIE.

A CRYING SHAME!

"Daily Express" Correspondent.

PLYMOUTH, Thursday.

The greatest indignation prevails among the inhabitants of Plymouth because of the astonishing freedom given to conscientious objectors who are now at Dartmoor, and Mr. J. P. Goldsmith, the mayor, has been asked to call a public meeting to protest against the Government regulations which permit these shirkers to flaunt themselves openly in so important a naval base.

Alderman Woolcombe is one of the leaders in the agitation, and he has the support of every man and woman in Plymouth in the demand he is making for a more rigorous treatment of the eight hundred conscientious objectors who are in the famous convict prison.

As a matter of fact, many of the objectors are leading a more enjoyable life at Dartmoor than they were when following their ordinary vocations outside. It will surprise people to learn that conscientious objectors on leave are actually driven about Plymouth and district for joy rides in motorcars supplied by their friends, and naturally the assumption is that the money to pay for the hire of these cars comes from certain pro-German sources in London.

THE DARTMOOR DO-NOTHINGS.—Alongside the map of the region across which our citizen soldiers are driving the hosts of militarism and barbarism it is fitting at the moment to exhibit these typical faces of "men" who have refused to do their share of the fighting and who by their levity and idleness on Dartmoor are rousing keen resentment both on the spot and in Parliament. [Exclusive "Daily Mail" Photograph.

"PEACE" WHEN THERE IS NO PEACE.—While our "Tommies" are fighting and bleeding in France, and our hospital ships are being sunk, the Dartmoor "conscience" youths are allowed to be grinning peace demonstrators. To-day their manner of life will be the subject of searching questions in the House of Commons. ["Daily Mail" Photograph.

In April 1917 the *Daily Mail* and local press whipped up public hatred against the conscientious objectors at Princetown Work Camp, Dartmoor, accusing them of living lives of luxury and being 'Dartmoor Do-Nothings' while brave soldiers died in the trenches. As a result many COs in Princetown were attacked and vilified by local people. Cyril Heasman's album, with thanks to Naomi Rumball.

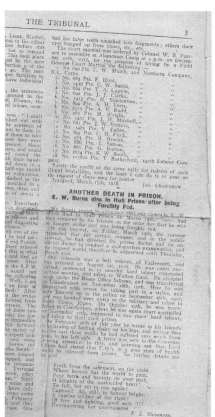

THE TRIBUNAL

ANOTHER DEATH IN PRISON.
E. W. Burns dies in Hull Prison after being
Forcibly Fed.

Left: Article in the *Tribunal*, 23 March 1918, recording the death of W.E. Burns who died in Hull Prison as a result of being forcibly fed. He choked when the liquid food went into his lungs. Cyril Heasman's album, with thanks to Naomi Rumball.

Below: 'Souvenir' postcard showing scenes from the Home Office work camps and settlements. Cyril Heasman's album, with thanks to Naomi Rumball.

Conscientious objectors posing for a photograph at Princetown Work Centre, Dartmoor. Cyril Heasman's album, with thanks to Naomi Rumball.

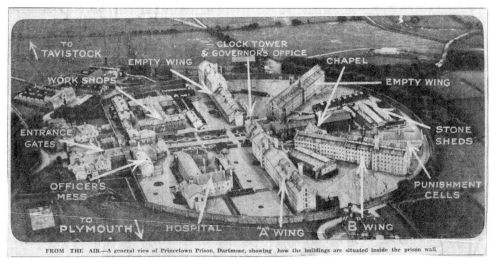

Aerial view of Princetown Prison or work centre, Dartmoor, showing the various buildings. Cyril Heasman's album, with thanks to Naomi Rumball.

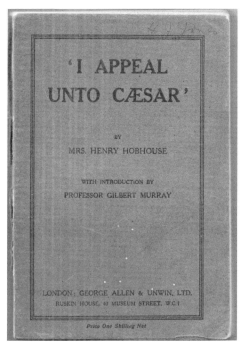

Cover of '*I Appeal unto Caesar*' by Mrs Henry Hobhouse, mother of Stephen Hobhouse who was imprisoned as a conscientious objector. Mrs Hobhouse had considerable influence and her campaign contributed to the release of 300 seriously weakened and ill conscientious objectors in December 1917.

A wooden plaque carved in memory of the seventy-three conscientious objectors who died as a result of brutal treatment in prison or home office centres. It was originally carved in Britain. In 1924 it was set up in the Berlin headquarters of the German League of War Resisters. In 1933 it was taken to Denmark and in 1940 hidden in a cellar. Recovered after the Second World War it was given to the Peace Pledge Union in 1959 and still hangs on the PPU's office wall. With thanks to the Peace Pledge Union.

Peet and Meyer arrived to hear that the COs had been warned that continued disobedience would result in the death sentence. According to Peet:

A personally conducted tour at the hands of the War Office meant that we were only able to see what the authorities wanted us to see … I was allowed no communication with the men, although … I was allowed to shake hands with four I knew personally. Dr Meyer was allowed to speak briefly to the prisoners in the presence of the Commandant …

The COs were court-martialled on the 10, 12 and 13 June. All men were tried by the Field General Court Martial, which had the power to issue the death penalty. A couple of days before his court martial Alfred Evans was approached by an army captain who told him that his papers were marked with 'death' in red and asked him whether Evans intended to go on with his protest. Evans replied that 'men are dying in the trenches for the things that they believe in and I wouldn't be less than them'. To Evan's astonishment, the captain stepped back, saluted him and shook his hand.

Knowing of the probability of the death sentence, Brocklesby had asked a fellow CO, a Jehovah's Witness named Leonard Renton, how far he was prepared to go. '"To the last ditch," said he and one by one they all said the same. It was the most thrilling experience of my life.' Stuart Beavis expressed much the same sentiments in a letter smuggled out to his mother in which he wrote: 'We have been warned to-day that we are now within the war zone, and the military authorities have absolute power, and disobedience may be followed by very severe penalties and very possibly the death penalty … Do not be downhearted if the worst comes to the worst; many have died cheerfully for a worse cause.'

On 15 June the first four COs – Howard Marten, H.W. Scullard, J.R. Ring and J. Foister – were taken out onto the parade ground to hear their sentences. Interviewed by the IWM, Howard Marten later described what happened:

There was a big concourse of men, mostly of the Non-Combatant Corps and the labour battalions, lined up in an immense square. We were taken to one side of it, and then under escort taken out one by one to the middle of the square. I was the first of them and until my verdict was known, nobody knew exactly what was going to happen. Then an officer in charge of the proceedings read out the various crimes and misdemeanours: refusing to obey a lawful command, disobedience at Boulogne and so on … then, 'The sentence of the court is to suffer death by being shot.' Then there was a suitable pause. And one thought 'Well that's that.' And then … 'Confirmed by the Commander in Chief.' That's double sealed it now. Then another long pause, 'But subsequently commuted to penal servitude for ten years.' And that was that …

Brocklesby, Murfin and others were waiting to hear what was happening, when a corporal rushed in saying that four COs from Field Punishment Barracks had been sentenced to death, commuted to ten years. Subsequently, Brocklesby, Murfin and various other COs were taken through the same procedure, with the same results.

In all thirty-five of the fifty conscientious objectors were marched out onto the parade ground, sentenced to death and then informed the sentence was commuted to ten years' penal servitude. Writing about his experience, one conscientious objector said:

As I stood listening to the sentences of the rest of our party, the feeling of joy and triumph surged up within me, and I felt proud to

COs sentenced to death

Thirty-five conscientious objectors were sentenced to death in France in 1916. The sentence was commuted to ten years' hard labour. The men were: Cornelius Barritt; Stuart Beavis; Bernard Bonner; H.F. Brewster; John (Bert) Brocklesby; Clifford Cartwright; E.C. Cryer; Alfred Evans; Jack Foster; W.T. Frear; Norman Gaudie; Clarence Hall; Stafford Hall; Geoffrey Hicks; Rowland Jackson; P.B. Jordan; Herbert Law; William Law; R.A. Lown; Howard Marten; Alfred Martlew; Frederick Murfin; Alfred Myers; Adam Priestly; Leonard Renton; Oscar Ricketts; John Ring; John Routledge; Harry Scullard; Herbert Senior; Ernest Spencer; Harold Stanton. Alfred Tayler; Edwin Walker; A.F. Walling.

have the privilege of being one of that small company of C.O.s testifying to a truth which the world as yet had not grasped, but which it would one day treasure as a most precious inheritance.

News of the death sentences, albeit commuted to long prison sentences, caused some outrage in Britain. It did not gain support from

'We will not cease'

New Zealand introduced conscription in 1916 with extremely limited provision for conscientious objection. Nevertheless, there were COs who were prepared to brave brutality and imprisonment to maintain their stand. In July 1917 a group of fourteen New Zealand conscientious objectors was sent to Britain on board the troopship *Waitemata*. Among them were Mark Briggs, Archibald Baxter and his brothers Alexander and John. The New Zealand authorities were determined to break the fourteen men who were considered to be particularly recalcitrant. The men experienced extreme brutality, which began as they boarded the ship, Briggs and others being dragged up the gangplank for refusing to walk. Once on board the men were stripped, placed in uniform and confined. The journey lasted three weeks and there was no provision for seasickness. When the men refused uniforms, they were stripped naked and left on deck in front of other passengers. Arriving at Sling Camp in Britain, they continued to refuse orders and were placed in solitary confinement. In October 1917 a group, including Baxter and Briggs, was sent to Etaples in France, subjected to repeated sentences of Field Punishment No. 1 and then forced into the trenches. All of them were continuously beaten and denied food; some, among them Baxter and Briggs, were dragged by ropes through water and over duckboards, nails scratching their skin, to force them into the front line. Baxter was placed on his own in an area that was constantly shelled. In the face of such appalling treatment, most of the men gave up their resistance but Baxter and Briggs held out to the end. In 1939 Baxter wrote an account of his experiences, *We Will Not Cease*.

the British public – the Battle of the Somme with its horrendous casualties was imminent and few had sympathy for COs – but it proved once and for all not just that the army could not break their resistance but also that objectors would have died for their principles.

Soon after sentencing the objectors, or 'Frenchmen' as they became known, were sent first to the military prison in Rouen, where they continued resisting orders, and were subsequently sent back to Britain to start their prison sentences.

Chapter 6

Prison

'They put me in for killing and they put you in for refusing to kill'
Lifer to conscientious objector

More than 6,000 conscientious objectors were arrested for failing to obey an army call-up notice or for ignoring the direction to take up civilian work. Some 5,970 were court-martialled and sent to prison. The usual procedure was that COs were arrested by the police at their place of work or from home. They were then taken in front of a magistrate court, fined – most COs refused to pay their fines – and escorted to an army barracks and put in the guardroom. How long they spent in the guardroom varied considerably from a night to a few weeks. They were then handed over to the army, where they refused orders, were court-martialled and given a prison sentence. Initially, COs were placed in military detention but from May 1916 they were sent to civilian prisons – possibly because the authorities thought conscientious objectors would 'infect' soldiers with their views. Conditions in prison varied but were in the main harsh and intimidating: archaic rules, poor food, meaningless tasks and long stretches of silence, isolation and boredom caused physical and mental damage, driving many objectors to the very limits of their endurance. Some objectors – the hard-core absolutists – endured two, three or more periods of imprisonment, some being incarcerated for three years.

Arrests
The arrests began almost within days of conscription being introduced. On 6 April 1916 under a heading 'The Persecution Begins', the *Tribunal* reported that N-CF members around the country were being arrested,

fined and handed over to the military. On 20 April the paper reported that it had received details of more than thirty N-CF members who had been arrested as absentees. By 27 May nearly 700 objectors had been arrested and by the end of July, the number had risen to 1,715. Between the end of July 1916 and the beginning of 1917 more than 3,000 COs were arrested and by March 1918 the figure was over 5,000. By January 1919, according to the *Tribunal*, more than 6,100 objectors had been arrested.

Wilfred Littleboy was arrested at the end of 1916. His tribunal had sent him into non-combatant service. He refused to turn up on the allotted day and knew he would be arrested but carried on as usual, living with the knowledge that 'you might be picked up at any time'. On the last day of 1916, a Sunday, he found police waiting at his home. He was arrested and appeared in court on the Monday morning. The magistrate handed him over to the military authorities: 'I was taken by escort to the military barracks at Warwick and placed in the guardroom. Within a day or two a uniform was placed in front of me and I was told to put it on … I said I did not regard myself as a soldier and had no intention of putting it on.' Littleboy was duly court-martialled and sentenced to 112 days hard labour in Wormwood Scrubs.

Harsh sentences
With the exception of the 'Frenchmen' who were sentenced to 10 years' hard labour, COs were usually sentenced to between 112 days and 2 years' hard labour. The latter was the harshest sentence on the statute book, short of hanging or life imprisonment. The risks to physical and mental well being of such a long sentence under such conditions were very high and a number of senior judges protested, saying that they had never given such sentences. However, in the eyes of the courts martial, conscientious objectors were cowards and shirkers; they deserved severe punishments, an approach that chimed with Lloyd George's statement, when as Secretary of State for War, he said in June 1916 that when it came to absolutists: 'that kind of man I personally have no sympathy for whatsoever … I shall only consider the best means of making the path of that class as hard as possible'.

Conscientious objectors were sent to various civilian prisons around the country, including Wormwood Scrubs, Wandsworth, Pentonville, Walton Prison, Liverpool, Durham, Maidstone and Winchester. Harold

Bing, who served time in Wormwood Scrubs and Winchester Prison, remembered that:

> Conditions in the civilian prisons varied a good deal. Some prisons had a reputation for being fairly lenient; others for being very harsh. Winchester Prison had a reputation for being a very harsh prison … some of the men who were brought back from France in the early summer of 1916 were taken to Winchester Prison before being transferred to Maidstone Prison … which was a prison for long-term prisoners and I did hear that a number of those prisoners got badly treated.

Reception

Having been taken to prison – Fenner Brockway was taken in a horse-drawn Black Maria – objectors were escorted through a series of locked doors and taken into the reception area. Once inside, an objector was questioned, told to strip, given a physical examination, told to bathe and hand over his normal clothes. The objector was given a prison uniform and eventually taken to his cell.

William Joseph (Will) Chamberlain was the editor of the N-CF's *Tribunal* until July 1916 when he was imprisoned, together with Fenner Brockway, Clifford Allen and other members of the N-CF committee, for publishing a leaflet, 'Repeal the Act'. The leaflet contravened the Defence of the Realm Act (DORA), which was introduced shortly after the war began. Refusing to pay their fines, the men surrendered to the police at Mansion House on Monday July 17 and were sentenced to sixty-one days in Pentonville Prison. According to a report in the *Tribunal* on 20 July, they were accompanied by many friends and were in excellent spirits. In his account *A C.O. In Prison*, Chamberlain somewhat light-heartedly describes different aspects of his prison experience, including the men's arrival.

> We make our way across the yard and reach a door euphemistically labelled 'Reception'. Through the door and into a small, bare room containing a desk and a number of forms, and we are in the 'Body-receiving' department of the prison! Here we sit upon a form while an officer enters us into the books … We next pass into a long room with small cells, just large enough for one person, ranged on either side. In the centre of the room are hot-water pipes, scales and two

desks, with a warder at each. Here full particulars of each prisoner are entered into more books. It is a very tedious process, as not only ourselves, but every article of clothing, money, watch and chain, etc., has to be separately noted. This done we are weighed and measured, and passed into the bathroom. Here we are ordered to strip and place all our clothes in a heap on the floor. We then wade through the bath (it might have been clean enough, but it did not look so hence the wade!) and on stepping out at the other end we discover our prison clothes awaiting us. The outfit consists of flannel vest and pants, cotton shirt, socks, a large coarse handkerchief, and the regulation 'uniform' of dull khaki stamped with thick, black broad-arrows.

Chamberlain describes himself and his friends as a 'merry party', which they probably were given they were young men, certain of their beliefs, and entered prison as a confident group with a lot of support but the lightness of his writing provides few clues as to just how harsh prison was. He was not alone in this: several COs recorded their prison experiences in writing or interviews; listening to the interviews their voices recount dreadful experiences in a very matter-of-fact way. Many seem to make light of their personal difficulties, perhaps because so many felt an obligation not to complain when men who had chosen a different path to them were suffering in the trenches. COs were, after all, honourable men. However, the impact of prison was profound; conscientious objectors were essentially political prisoners who had no previous experience of prison or its conditions. Their previous lives had been very different from the other prisoners, many of whom were inside for murder, theft or other crimes. Harold Bing was to spend nearly three years in prison but, as he says: 'I don't think I had any knowledge of what prison was like before I went in. I had met one or two people who had been in prison briefly but never spoke to them about prison.' Not surprisingly, as the war and the COs' resistance continued, they came to know the conditions only too well.

One of the effects of prison was to undermine a man's sense of identity. In 'Prisoners for Peace', Fred Murfin, who had been sentenced to death in France, commuted to ten years' penal servitude, described arriving at Winchester Prison on 7 July 1916, to begin his sentence:

We were all put into a reception room. There was the usual medical examination and our particulars were taken. Then we were led away to become a number. I was C3/31 i.e. No 31 on the third landing of 'C' Hall. A disc was worn on the coat front with the cell number on. A change of cell meant a change of disc. This was our means of identity.

Hubert Peet too in his account of his first prison sentence, *112 Days' Hard Labour*, which appeared as a supplement to the Quaker newspaper the *Ploughshare* in 1917, describes how being given a prison number was 'only another aspect of the absence of opportunity for self-expression'.

Another of the 'Frenchmen' who arrived in Winchester was John Brocklesby. According to his memoir, there were around 60 'conshies [*sic*]' in Winchester, including Murfin, Stuart Beavis and Cornelius Barritt, nicknamed 'Corney'. When it came to giving the men their prison clothes, the warders could not find clothes large enough for Brocklesby. The trousers caused a particular problem: they were either wide enough or too short, or long enough and too tight. Ultimately, he ended up with trousers that came half way up his calves, something that apparently caused considerable 'merriment'. According to Murfin: 'We had a bit of humour occasionally. The prison uniform wasn't smart and Bert Brocklesby, who was six feet tall, was fitted out with trousers at least one foot short. On exercise he was showing off, so that everyone noticed and enjoyed the sight. That was soon altered.'

In their personal accounts many COs comment on the fact that humour helped them to get through the weeks, months and even years that they spent locked away. In reality, the conditions were appalling, not just for conscientious objectors but for ordinary prisoners as well, so much so that Quaker Hubert Peet and socialist Fenner Brockway later collaborated on a report, *English Prisons Today*. Published in 1922, the report helped to initiate much-needed prison reform.

Cells

Prisoners were kept in single cells 11ft x 14ft x 7ft. The floor was of square tiles or rough black concrete, walls were brick and there was a small window high up so that a prisoner needed to stand on a stool to look out. It was however forbidden to look out of the window. A spyhole in the door enabled warders to look in. On one occasion journalist Hubert Peet, secretary of the Friends' Service Committee, was spied on while saying his prayers and accused of using 'foul language' by the warder.

Describing his cell, Harold Bing said:

I was in a cell by myself the whole time … [it] was about 6ft by 13ft with one small window above one's head so you couldn't see out of it except by standing on your stool, which you might be punished for. In your door was a little spy hole with a cover on the outside, so the warder could come along and spy on you at any time to see what you were up to so you had the sense of being watched the whole time … gave you a very uncomfortable feeling at first until in time you got used to it. In the cell was a plank bed, which was stood up against the door during the day and put down at night with a mattress. For the first month you were not allowed a mattress, you slept on the bare plank boards. At the end of a month you were given a mattress. In addition you had two or three blankets and a pillow. There was also a small table and stool, a chamber pot, a can for water and a metal bowl in which to wash and a small shelf on which one kept one's knife, spoon and fork, a pot of salt and any photographs which one was allowed to have. One was normally permitted not to have more than 2 or 3 photographs and they must be members of one's family or close relatives.

English prisons had the wooden plank beds that Bing describes; in Scottish prisons, a stone slab served as a bed. Cell floors were of tiles or black concrete. Knives were made of bendable tin, making them impossible aids to suicide. Photographs were not allowed until a hard labour prisoner had served four months. Food was handed into the cells in a tin, which according to Fred Murfin was often dirty. A list of prison regulations was attached to the wall; there were severe punishments for breaking rules.

Cells had little or no heating and during the winter could become intolerably cold. A conscientious objector's wife wrote that when she met her husband coming out of prison one February, she was horrified to see how badly he was suffering from the cold.

His face showed this very much, and in addition to this his hands were literally covered with chilblains … painted with iodine … he said that 'that was nothing to what they had been'. He also told me that for the last few weeks it had been so cold that he had been quite unable to read … he could only pace up and down his cell …

normally he does not feel the cold at all … I have never known him to have a chilblain …

Cold and damp conditions meant that many objectors suffered from colds, influenza, tuberculosis and bronchitis.

Conversely, during warm weather cells became unbearably hot and airless. Sometimes prisoners fainted in their cells and were not discovered until the morning. One CO, waiting for a court martial and inevitable second prison term, wrote:

> I have seen a man go raving mad in the prison after being shut up in a warm cell from 4 o'clock in the afternoon until 6 o'clock the next morning. The cells are very badly ventilated, the one I was in had all the windows fastened down … Some cells have two little windows … but some have not, and it gets very hot … especially when the sun is beating in, it gets unbearable. I have seen cell doors opened in the morning, and the men stretched out on the floor in fits or panting, and the warders do not take any notice of them but simply pass on and leave the door open …

The first month for prisoners on hard labour was particularly difficult. Apart from the lack of a mattress, they were not allowed any letters, visits or books, other than the Bible, prayer book and one 'educational' book. They were also confined to their cells for more than 23 hours out of every 24, apart from a brief period for exercise, so had absolutely no communication with the outside world.

Once new arrivals had been processed, the librarian gave them one 'educational' book, which they could read in their cell. It had to last a month and prisoners had no say in the choice. Ironically, Will Chamberlain was presented with *The Fifteen Decisive Battles of the World*.

After the first month prisoners were allowed to work 'in association'; this might mean sitting working in the corridor outside their cells, or in the prison workshops, or in outdoor working parties. After two months prisoners were allowed to send and receive one letter a month and to have a monthly visit. Those writing to prisoners were told to keep letters short and not to include information about current events. Prisoners were forbidden to write about prison conditions or other prisoners, which as time went on could make filling a letter very difficult. As Harold Bing described:

> For those of us who were too far from home to be able to receive any visitors, an arrangement was made by which we could have an extra letter … in the latter time of my time in prison I was writing a letter home … and receiving a reply once a fortnight … letters were limited in length and strictly censored and you were not allowed to mention anything that happened in prison, which by the end of two years made it very difficult to fill a letter at all. You were supposed only to discuss domestic matters and for an unmarried man who had been in prison for two years, there were very few domestic matters that you could discuss.

Visits from family or friends were eagerly anticipated but any kind of privacy was impossible, which could make a visit stressful, as Fred Murfin remembered: 'I had one visit. It was a tremendous strain on both my parents and myself. There was a wire partition in front of both parties and a space between, where a Warder listened to all that was said.' Warders varied though and some were more sympathetic than others, trying to keep a tactful distance. Both letters and visits were however seen as privileges and could be instantly removed if a prisoner broke rules. On one occasion John Brocklesby's father and fiancée arrived, having travelled 400 miles to visit him, but the visit was refused because Brocklesby was being punished for refusing to do prison work. In this case, however, Brocklesby's father, who was a JP, said the refusal was illegal and the visit went ahead.

Routine
The prison day began at 5.30am when prisoners were woken and taken out to the lavatories to wash and empty the latrine pail – slopping out. They then had to scrub their cells and furniture and fold their bedding according to prison regulations. Breakfast was at 6am; it consisted of one pint of unsweetened porridge, 8oz of bread and ¼oz of margarine. As Murfin asked: 'Have you ever tried to spread ¼ ounce of margarine on 8 ounces of bread? Breakfast was followed by 30–45 minutes of supervised exercise, either circling the prison yard or, if the weather

was bad, walking around the corridors. Talking was forbidden. Then came work, which included sewing mailbags, making mats or breaking stones. Lunch was at midday and typically consisted of potatoes, bread, green beans and fat heavy bacon. The meat content varied, depending on the day: corned beef on Sunday; beans and fat bacon on Monday; braised beef on Tuesday; beef stew on Wednesday; mutton on Thursday and Friday; and suet pudding on Saturday. After lunch, the men worked until about 4.15pm or 4.30pm when they were returned to their cells and ate their final meal of the day: bread, margarine and, after four months in prison, one pint of cocoa, slightly sweetened. From 4.30pm in the evening until 5.30am the next morning, the men were locked in their cells. If books were available, they read or the men just lost themselves in thought. The only break in routine was on Sunday when prisoners were allowed out to attend chapel.

Hunger was a constant: the prison diet was incredibly meagre and designed to reduce energy. Most conscientious objectors experienced a considerable amount of weight loss as well as lethargy, insomnia, headaches and other related disorders. However, not only was the food inadequate it also contained dirt, insects and evidence of vermin. One conscientious objector recorded that:

The rice invariably disclosed the fact that there must be a swarm of mice in the prison kitchen or store. This tended to sicken one, although low feeding made me proof even against this – I had a black beetle in my mouth one day. This ... was an exception, yet I mentioned it to a warder, and he told me not to say anything ... because the other prisoners may ask for them too. Yet the mice's dirt was the rule, and never a day passed when we had rice but that I picked out half a dozen or more lumps of evidence.

'For each meal there were potatoes, cooked in their jackets and generally dirty. Occasionally there was cabbage. One year, in the summer, there was a generous supply of caterpillars. Once or twice a year a coarse Cos lettuce, just as it was pulled up, and spring onions, also dirty, were thrown into the cell.'

Fred Murfin

When they first came into prison many conscientious objectors found it almost impossible to eat the prison food but eventually hunger overcame distaste and squeamishness. The nature of the diet caused problems for vegetarians, such as Harold Bing:

> When I first went into prison, one ate the rest of the food and left the meat and the meat went back in the food tin to the kitchen. In Winchester I found it was possible, a sort of smuggling arrangement, to exchange my meat for potatoes with the prisoner in the next cell and I did this for some time.

Eventually, a ruling came down from the Home Office that those who applied for vegetarian diet should be allowed it; as rationing intensified even COs who had not been vegetarian when they came into prison applied for it, thinking it would be preferable. Once this happened, however, prison authorities refused new applications for vegetarian diets.

Work

Prison work was dull, monotonous and soul-destroying. According to Harold Bing:

> For the most part when I was in the cell, I was engaged in making mail bags and later on in Winchester … I worked in the twining shop, making rope and twine for post office purposes … at the end of the first month one is supposed to work in association … you go into a big workshop where you are working together on making mailbags, or picking oakum or making rope … Prison work is manual work, very repetitive, very boring and seems to be designed chiefly to keep one occupied with work as uninteresting as it can be.

Fenner Brockway too wrote about sewing mailbags in his account *Inside the Left*:

> The minimum task of mail bag sewing was seventy feet a day. We sewed with large needles which looked like skewers, pressing them through the canvas by a lead knob strapped to the palm of our hands. At first the seventy feet … seemed an impossible task; working hard I could get done only thirty feet in ten hours … Before

the end of my prison experience the seventy feet seemed like child's play; I could do it in four hours.

George Dutch was another who soon mastered the skill: 'I got proficient at making mail bags. I used to do my quota and a bit over and was rewarded with a mug of ship's cocoa and a hunk of bread which was very welcome because the diet was very poor. Much worse than the army diet and I was a vegetarian ...'

As time passed, objectors were moved onto other tasks, such as working in the prison gardens, the library or in one of the various workshops. Work such as this was seen as a privilege and objectors were frequently punished by being taken out of workshops.

Reading offered an escape from prison life but books were scarce. After the first two months, prisoners could change their 'educational' book once a month, and take another from the prison library. They were also allowed one novel. The choice of books in the library was limited but after a while a concession was made that if prisoners wanted books for study purposes only, they could ask their friends to send books provided these books became part of the prison library. Not surprisingly COs seized the opportunity and a number of books were sent in, including some history books that Bing requested, although, as he found, 'one's power of concentration tends to decrease after long months in prison ... your eyes had passed over the letters but the contents hadn't entered your brain at all'.

Silence and resistance

Prisoners were forbidden to talk to anyone; they could not speak to other prisoners or to the warders, unless the warder asked them a question. Whether in their cells, at work or in the exercise yard, silence was the rule. For Quaker John Graham, who served as a Quaker chaplain to objectors in Manchester Gaol, the silence rule was 'hideous'. For Hubert Peet, 'The attempted imposition of silence is unmoral, even if not immoral; the isolation drives the man into himself and tempts him at every turn to fulfil the human instinct of communication with his fellows, a course only possible by the exercise of some petty deceit or the breaking of a rule.' Silence combined with isolation and the attempt to destroy personal identity could shatter a man, and some COs did go mad in prison.

Fenner Brockway considered that the prison system was 'absolutely inhuman and denying human rights. We were not even allowed to speak to each other. Of course we did but we always had the sense of doing something which was prohibited and which if we were found doing would lead to punishment – bread and water, solitary confinement.'

Punishment for breaking rules was severe: as Brockway described, a bread and water diet for men who were already weakened by poor diet and solitary confinement, usually in dark, dank cells. But as Brockway emphasised 'as always in prison we were able to defeat regulations'. During exercise periods, hiding the sounds with the noise of their boots, objectors managed to exchange a few words with each other, sometimes quietly, sometimes quite openly, greeting each other, passing on news, and even cracking jokes, something, according to Will Chamberlain that often nearly gained them the punishment cells.

Objectors developed some extraordinarily ingenious methods of communicating with each other. On arrival in Walton Prison, Fenner Brockway was surreptitiously given a sheet of lavatory paper on which was written a 'telephone code', a form of Morse code with dots and dashes for each letter of the alphabet. Using this code and tapping on the hot water pipe that ran through the cells, objectors were able to communicate with each other, each objector having his own 'telephone number', which was the number of his cell. Warders in the corridors could not hear the sounds because the pipe was actually in the cells and effectively soundproofed by the thick doors and walls. In this way, objectors could 'talk' to teach other, passing on news from the N-CF, holding meetings and discussions. Objectors even used this method to play chess. While he was in Winchester Prison, Clifford Allen played chess matches with Scott Ducker, a solicitor, who was five cells down the corridor. Apparently, the two of them organised a coded chess tournament involving several objectors.

Secret 'newspapers'

Objectors were nothing if not inventive in their challenges to the system and their attempts to subvert it. They were not allowed any writing materials, other than paper and pencils for writing letters, something that Hubert Peet, as a journalist used to noting down thoughts and observations, found intolerable. The paper was rationed and pencils taken away. They were however given coarse brown-grey sheets of lavatory paper every day. Using these and pencil leads smuggled into prison by new arrivals, objectors in every prison secretly managed to produce tiny 'newspapers', which were circulated among the comrades. It was an extraordinary achievement, not just because of the time and effort involved and the secrecy needed but also because the cells were regularly searched by warders; if anything had been discovered there would have been serious repercussions. COs read issues of the prison papers with enthusiasm, passing them from one to another. The prison lavatory was an obvious place to read the journals. On one occasion so many COs were queuing to read that the warden asked someone to find out what the food had been that day.

The underground papers included the *Canterbury Clinker*, which was published fortnightly by Barratt Brown and included verse, poetry and studies in ethics; the *Joyland Journal*, produced in Montjoy Prison, Dublin, a very artistic publication, which included sketches, cartoons, headlines, a serial and was cloth bound; the *Instigilo*, written entirely in Esperanto and produced at Dorchester Prison; the *Walton Leader*, which was produced by Fenner Brockway and ran to 100 issues, only being discovered once; and the *Winchester Court Martial*, which was entirely devoted to humour and although not much larger than a bus ticket, was neatly written and designed to look like a smart newspaper. Produced by Will Chamberlain, it only ran to four issues because Chamberlain became ill. It was succeeded by the *Winchester Whisperer*, which was produced fortnightly or, as the byline announced, 'post-searchly'.

Interviewed in 1974, Harold Bing remembered the ingenious methods they used:

Some prisoners managed to make little inkwells by taking a block of cobblers wax, which was used to make mail bags … making a hole in it, sinking a thimble into the wax, and covering it up with another piece of wax so what appeared to be a block of wax, was in fact a block of wax with a lid and when you lifted the lid, there was a thimble, and that thimble you filled with ink … with inkpots of that kind there was produced in Winchester Prison a periodical called the Winchester Whisperer. It was written on small brown sheets of toilet paper … people wrote little essays or poems, humorous remarks, sometimes little cartoons or pictures and all these pieces of paper were passed surreptitiously from hand to hand and reached the editor who bound them together … and this issue … was then passed round secretly hidden under people's waistcoats or up their sleeves and, as it happened, despite many searches, no copy of that issue was ever captured by the warders … all the copies were finally smuggled out and placed in some depository in London …

There is one copy of the *Winchester Whisperer* in the Quaker Library in London – it was published on 21 December 1918. Nearly 100 years old, it is very fragile and has to be handled very carefully. The issue consists of 100 tiny pages of lavatory paper, bound with a piece of hessian sacking and is embroidered on the cover. About 5in square, it contains an editorial, articles, drawings, poems, jokes, cartoons, letters to the editor, a chess corner and 'For the Chicks by Uncle Toby', which lampoons the election process. The title page shows a picture of a CO working in prison, overlooked by a warder. Inside another drawing shows two soldiers – one British, one German – on the 'crucifix' – Field Punishment No. 1, with two capitalists holding bowls into which blood streams out from the sides of the soldiers. The caption reads: 'English

After the war, the N-CF published the *C.O. Clink Chronicle*, which included extracts from the COs' prison journals; it was effectively a mini-anthology. One of the pieces included came from the *Winchester Court Martial* and was written by Will Chamberlain:

Great British Victory
Our special correspondent at the back of the front reports that in the early hours of Sunday last the British captured a cowshed. Our losses were only 10,000. The enemy losses must be at least 100,000.

It is hoped that this splendid victory will stop the cry for peace, which seems to have taken hold of a large section of the British people.

In the early hours of Monday the enemy made a strong counter-attack and recaptured the above cowshed. Their losses are estimated at 250,000; our casualties were practically nil.

The cowshed is of no military value.

Tommy. Well Fritz they say we've won! But to take my life blood as well as yours.' The date of the issue indicates, as was the case, that absolutists were not released from prison until well after the Armistice. As the different writing on the pages show there were a number of contributors, each with their own individual style. It is remarkable to think of the objectors producing this unique publication under such difficult situations, but it was truly a successful example of subversive ingenuity. Producing papers in secret and keeping them away from the warders was not just remarkable but also subversive.

Resistance and solitary confinement
After a while, Brockway, who was one of the leading members of the N-CF, decided the time had come to challenge the system openly:

A point came when many of us felt that it was undignified and humiliating to accept the system itself and we decided openly to resist it. For ten glorious days sixty of us ran our own hall in prison. Speaking openly on the exercise ground instead of marching five steps behind each other and not saying a word – round and round. We took arms, we played games, we organised concerts every night. We were shut in our cells but at the window were lots of Welsh boys who could sing beautifully; they would sing at the window and everybody down the side could hear. But the effect became disastrous at Walton Prison in Liverpool because not only could our own boys hear but the ordinary prisoners heard as well. And so the five leaders were isolated and then we were transferred to other prisons.

Brockway was transferred to Lincoln Prison and as punishment was given eight months in solitary confinement. For the first three months he was kept on a bread and water diet, until finally the doctor ended it. Despite this treatment, Brockway said that he 'had a sense of freedom which I can't describe … The Governor would summon me to his presence and instead of … standing at attention … I would say "Good morning governor, nice morning isn't it?" One had an extraordinary sense of personal liberty, personal freedom.'

An interesting thing happened to Brockway while he was in Lincoln. Sinn Fein leaders, including de Valera, were also in the prison:

They got to hear I was there ... I was in a cell alone 23 hours and 20 minutes out of 24 shut in the cell, 40 minutes exercise on my own. Anyway they got to know I was there and one day I heard a step outside my cell, got up on my stool and looked outside and there was a red band man ... a prisoner who was allowed to go about without warders. He signalled to me to get down and through the opening came a message from the Sinn Feiners: 'Just heard you're here. We can do anything for you except get you out. Let us know what you want.' I ordered a daily newspaper. I got the *Guardian* every day. I ordered a weekly paper. I got the *Labour Leader*, which was being edited in my absence.

Brockway also received the *New Statesman*, the *Economist* and the *Observer*, smuggled to him by the red band man who collected them from the Sinn Fein latrines and placed them in the drain near Brockway's latrine. They were then smuggled back. They were not found because, Brockway being in solitary confinement, the warders never bothered to search his cell. In Brockway's opinion, the Sinn Fein 'saved my mind in that period of long solitary confinement'.

Brockway was not the only objector to undergo solitary confinement on a diet of bread and water. All the absolutists experienced it at one time or another. Via the 'telephone system', Murfin, Brocklesby and others were told the mailbags they were sewing were for military use, so they stopped work. According to Murfin:

Bert Brocklesby went on exercise and told all he could and said 'I've stopped work'. 'So have I,' I replied. We were reported to the Governor ... I got two days punishment – solitary confinement in a punishment cell, on only bread and water. These cells were on ground level, never cleaned out and were awful. There was a stool to sit on and one was for allowed for toilet once a day [*sic*]. Each night clothing was taken outside. There was just a bed board to lie on and no mattress.

Once back in his usual cell, Murfin spoke to other COs outside who were wondering where he had been. He was reported once more and was this time punished for 'shouting out of the window' and refusing to do the work: 'This resulted in three days of solitary confinement on bread and water.' Toward the end of 1917 a conscientious objector called Harold Blake was given eight months' solitary confinement for refusing to sew mailbags destined for the navy. He became gravely ill.

Cat and Mouse

Release from prison after serving a sentence did not mean the end of imprisonment for conscientious objectors. Once released, COs were still 'deemed' to be soldiers and were posted straight back to whichever army unit they had come from and once there, the whole business began again. Absolutist conscientious objectors once again refused orders, were placed in the guardroom, court-martialled and returned to prison to serve yet another sentence. The process mirrored the same 'cat and mouse' procedure that the government had imposed on suffragettes just a few years previously: like a cat playing with a mouse, suffragettes in poor health had been released from prison, then returned once their health was improved, to complete their sentences. Similarly, COs, though they had completed a sentence, were still part of the army and liable for further imprisonment if they continued to resist – which most of them did. Out of the 5,973 COs who were court-martialled and sent to prison, 655 were court-martialled twice; 521 three times; 319 four times; 50 five times; and 3 men went before courts-martial six times.

In the House of Commons in May 1939, MP Arthur Creech Jones, who served three terms of imprisonment as a First World War conscientious objector, described what had happened to him in an attempt to persuade the government of that time not to use the same methods against the second generation of 'conchies'. The following extract is taken from Hansard 16.4.39:

I went before a court martial and ... I was sentenced to a period of six months imprisonment with hard labour. I served my period ... and was then taken back to my regiment, given a military order, court-martialled afresh and sentenced to one year's hard labour. That sentence I also served, I was again taken back to my regiment, given another military order, refused to obey, was court-martialled again, and had to go for two years' hard labour. I served the two years' hard labour and went back to my regiment four months after the war was over. I still refused to obey military orders and was sentenced to another period of two years' hard labour ... It was recognised all through this course that I was a perfectly genuine person. Nevertheless I had been caught up in the military machine and the 'cat and mouse' arrangement began to operate.

Sense of purpose

Some of the letters written by conscientious objectors during the early months of prison indicate a strong sense of comradeship and unity of purpose. In February 1917 Fenner Brockway wrote:

> I am thoroughly well and I am happy. I do not seem to be in prison. You know how contentedly I entered; that feeling has remained … possessing that calmness within, the harshnesses which make prison prison don't seem to exist … I cannot describe to you the wonderful sense of comradeship there is among the C.O.s in prison. We are not allowed to speak to each other, but the unity we feel does not need expression in spirit … I went to chapel, the joy of being one of the eight hundred C.O.s there was almost intoxicating … You should have heard them sing … 'Give peace, O Lord, give peace again'. … I felt that such a body of men, nearly all quite young, could do much to answer the prayer of that hymn if they retain … their present enthusiasm … not merely to bring peace 'again' but for ever!

Clifford Allen also, in a long letter reproduced in full in John Graham's *Conscription and Conscience*, reflected on the differing emotions produced by being in prison, and, like Brockway, wrote about comradeship and sense of freedom experienced even though he was behind prison bars:

> The very fact that I can, as it were feel my bonds, gives me a more vivid consciousness of my real freedom. I can then see with unmistakable clearness the untold worth of what we are attempting … It does not matter then how many bars there are to my prison cell, or high the wall opposite my window … I seem to be in the closest contact with the other men shut away in their prison cells all over the country.

Repeated prison sentences were however to take their toll on the physical, and mental, well-being of the conscientious objectors but it is probably true to say that most lost this deep sense of purpose. The comradeship also, which comes across in all their writings, made it possible for them to continue their stand in a very hostile environment. In fact, as the months dragged on it became essential.

Chapter 7

Home Office Scheme

'I was driven to the absolute position by the Home Office Scheme.'
John Brocklesby

By summer 1916 the number of conscientious objectors being court-martialled and sent to prison was causing something of an embarrassment to the British government. As a result, a scheme was created whereby those conscientious objectors already in prison, and some who had not yet appeared before their tribunals, were to be re-examined and if found to be 'genuine' would be offered the opportunity to undertake work 'of national importance' in specially created work camps or prisons cleared for the purpose. The scheme was known as the Home Office Scheme.

On 28 June 1916, Prime Minister Asquith stood up in the House of Commons and, in a fairly long speech, explained the scheme to the assembled members:

> The procedure to be adopted, by the War Office in the cases of soldiers under Army Order X of May 25, 1916 sentenced to imprisonment for refusing to obey orders is as follows:
>
> > The first step is to sift out the cases where there is *prima-facie* evidence to show that the offence was the result of conscientious objection to military service. For this purpose all court martial proceedings on conscientious objectors will be referred for scrutiny to the War Office. With regard to the cases of those who have been before a Tribunal, the records will be consulted … With regard to those who have never been before a Tribunal, the first step will be to require them to answer the categorical questions

which the Tribunal might have put ... The men who are held to be genuine conscientious objectors will be released from the civil prison on their undertaking to perform work of national importance under civil control ... They will be transferred pro forma to Section W of the Army Reserve, and they will cease to be subject to military discipline or the Army Act so long as they continue to carry out satisfactorily the duties imposed upon them ...

So far, so apparently good, although Asquith completed his speech by saying that he was going to add two points which he thought would

meet with universal acceptance. The first is that all men whose objections to military service are founded on honest convictions ought to be able, and will be able, to avail themselves of the exemption which Parliament has provided; and, in the second place, it is necessary that men who put forward objections of this kind as a pretext and cloak to cover their indifference to the national call, and who are therefore guilty of the double offence of cowardice and hypocrisy, should be treated, as they ought to treated, with the utmost rigour.

Not surprisingly, loud cheers followed the last part of this statement as well as demands to deprive 'these men' of their civil rights, to inflict severe legal punishment and so on. Obviously, COs who refused to co-operate with the scheme, or who were rejected by the central tribunal would remain in prison.

Clearly, Asquith and others in the government and War Office felt that conscientious objectors would leap at this opportunity but, as usual, they had failed to understand the complexity and determination of conscientious objection, and what absolutist Harold Blake described as the 'inflexible and moral timbre' of the COs. Members of the Joint Advisory Council – Hubert Peet for the Friends Service Committee, Clifford Allen and Fenner Brockway for the N-CF and T. Hodgkin, chair of the FoR, wrote immediately to the government with their criticisms. For a start, they argued that as local tribunals had already failed to recognise that COs were genuine and sincere, why should a central tribunal, under the direction of the War Office, be any different? They also pointed out that any CO who failed the re-sifting process would automatically be labelled as a coward and a hypocrite and probably be treated more harshly than was already happening, and that absolutists, by definition, would refuse to enter into this 'bargain'.

Writing in the *Tribunal* on 6 July 1916, Clifford Allen stated their position:

> the Government's new proposal for dealing with conscientious objectors results from an entire misconception of our views and the character of our protest … there can be little doubt that that the new scheme will give rise to anger and resentment in the minds of many who deplore persecution but had withheld their protest in the hope that some way out would be discovered by Mr Asquith. As it is, the persecution will be intensified and brutality officially encouraged as the result of a proposal which disregards the stand already made by those who have been sentenced to death, penal servitude or other penalties. One might almost describe as ludicrous the proposal to institute a further enquiry into the genuineness of such conscientious objectors through the medium of the War Office, which is the last body in the world that can or ought to deal with such matters …

A few days previously he had already criticised the scheme for creating 'Battalions of Labour at sweated rates of pay' that would undermine the work of trade unions and bring wages down.

Subsequently, the N-CF committee wrote again to Asquith, spelling out the basic contradiction underpinning not just the scheme but also the whole approach towards conscientious objectors. Essentially, the government was proposing to release from prison men who agreed to work under civilian control and to continue punishing men who refused to accept the scheme. What the government did not seem to recognise, or did not want to recognise, was that there were conscientious objectors who could not and would not, because of their deeply held principles, accept anything that was imposed as part of the Military Service Act because any acceptance implied a compromise with militarism. The N-CF recognised there would be COs who would accept civilian work because they believed it was the right thing to do but this work should be work of 'real value to the community'. Instead, as the tribunal system existed work of so-called national importance was not giving COs the opportunity of 'rendering useful service to the community', but instead was 'inflicting some disability upon them in the name of what is called "equality of sacrifice"'. The letter went on to say that 'If work under civil control is to take the form of what amounts to a penalty instead of a service, it is bound to be rejected by men who would otherwise undertake it ...'.

Rejecting the scheme
The Home Office Scheme was run by a committee appointed by the Home Office under the chairmanship of William Brace MP. The Committee's full name was the Committee for the Employment of Conscientious Objectors. It should not be confused with the Pelham Committee and was quite a different animal.

It took a while to get the scheme up and running, not least because it was difficult for the Committee to find suitable work for COs who accepted the scheme. *The Times* in its inimitable fashion had insisted that men released from prison should be employed 'on a form of arduous and unremunerative public service' and there was a general feeling that COs on the scheme should be prepared to make sacrifices equal to those being suffered by men in the trenches. Eventually, the Committee managed to persuade the Road Board to employ up to 1,000 COs for road making and quarrying and the Home Grown Timber Committee agreed to take gangs of 30–40 men for forestry work. Llanelly Rural District Council also offered some work. Whether any of these jobs could have been described as work of national importance was another matter.

Towards the end of July a central tribunal was set up in Wormwood Scrubs and began interviewing conscientious objectors. Batches of COs were taken under escort to Wormwood Scrubs, each man appearing individually before the tribunal to have his case reviewed. The proceedings were brief, possibly not more than 3 minutes each and then COs were sent back to their prisons to wait for the decisions.

Just over 1,000 absolutists completely rejected the Home Office Scheme, even though it meant remaining in prison, subject to the cat and mouse procedure of continuing courts martial and prison sentences. Fenner Brockway and Clifford Allen rejected the scheme, as did Fred Murfin, Stuart Beavis and Alfred Taylor, who had been among the COs sent to France and sentenced to death. Harold Bing also rejected the Home Office scheme, explaining why in an interview with the IWM:

The government decided that cases would have to be reviewed and so sessions of the tribunal were held in Wormwood Scrubs prison ... They [conscientious objectors] were all sent to this central prison in London and they all had the opportunity of appearing before the central tribunal which, if it recognised them as genuine, in most cases it did ... offered them service under a scheme, what was called the Home Office Scheme, by which they could be transferred to a section of the Army Reserve and sent down to work on Dartmoor, from which the civil convicts had been removed. A considerable number of men accepted this scheme ... but a considerable number of us refused ... because it involved accepting a position in the Army Reserve with the possibility of call-up later on and because it was acknowledging the system of military conscription. ... Not only were we opposed to war, we were also opposed to conscription and could not therefore accept any service under a conscription act and those who took this line were those who became to be known as 'absolutists'. And about 1,000 men remained in prison for the greater part of the war and many of us for six months after the war.

Another who refused to accept the scheme was Harold Blake: 'To accept ANY condition of exemption from military service is to me equivalent to entering into a bargain with the government that, provided I am not required to do the killing, they can carry on with the war and kill as long and as hard as they like; and I am not prepared to make such a bargain.' Later, suffering dreadfully in prison and fearing he was going insane, he nearly weakened but had a dream in which his sister appeared as part of a heavenly choir. This strengthened his resolve.

Harold Bing found the experience of going in front of this tribunal-in-a-prison was very different from his previous two tribunals:

They said, 'We've got your papers; we see that you've been before the local and appeal tribunal, we see that the local tribunal granted you non-combatant service and the appeal tribunal was prepared to offer you work of national importance, therefore they had recognised you as genuine. Therefore, there's no need for us to go into that. Are you prepared to accept the Scheme?' And I declined. So I served three months in Wormwood Scrubs prison.

Accepting the scheme

Weakened and exhausted by prison and genuinely believing that they might indeed be put to some useful work, around 4,000 conscientious objectors accepted the scheme. One of them was John Brocklesby, who recorded in his memoirs that 'sometime in August, we were all moved to Wormwood Scrubs prison for about four days and had the opportunity to appear before the Central Tribunal. The examination was simple. Was I prepared to do work of national importance? I said I wanted to help the community but not the war.' Brocklesby was returned to Winchester and after a few days had corduroy working trousers issued to him. All those who accepted the scheme were issued with working clothes, some of which were quite extraordinary according to Harry Stanton, who was sent to Dyce work camp kitted out with corduroys, a peaked cap and a naval style waistcoat.

Scotsman Eric Dott, who became a doctor after the war, also accepted the scheme: 'When we'd done our 112 days hard labour at Wormwood Scrubs we were offered a choice of going to a place where we could do what was called "national importance" and have a certain amount of liberty there as long as we stayed in one of these centres like Dartmoor or Wakefield where they had made special arrangements.' Cyril Heasman also accepted the scheme. Born in Cheyne Walk in London, Heasman was an engraver and a member of the International Bible Students' Association, later the Jehovah's Witnesses. Aged 23, he appeared before his local tribunal in Wandsworth, where he stated his basis for conscientious objection as religious, saying, 'I cannot, as a Christian, take part in the war. I have sworn allegiance to the King of Kings. Christ's life was one of continual peace.' He was exempted from combatant service only and, like many other COs, refused to report for military service, which led to a court appearance and a fine. He was escorted to Kingston Barracks where he refused to put on a uniform, which led to his court martial. In January 1917 he was offered the Home Office Scheme, which he accepted. I was fortunate to interview Heasman's granddaughter, Naomi Rumball, who described her grandfather as a very charismatic and determined man. Unfortunately, there is no record of why her grandfather accepted the scheme but a good many Jehovah's Witnesses did do so and it is probable that he believed that he would achieve more by doing what many hoped would be useful work, than accepting a long prison sentence.

Another who accepted the scheme was Henry Sargent. Born and brought up in Hastings, Sargent was, according to his niece Margaret Sargent and close companion Mrs Susan Ronnie, a brilliant scholar, who specialised in natural history. He won a bursary to Hastings Art College and developed a keen interest in photography. After leaving college, he started work in Hastings Museum, which brought him into contact with a number of famous people, including Rudyard Kipling and the Jesuit priest, philosopher and naturalist Pierre Teilhard de Chardin, then studying theology in Hastings. According to his niece and Mrs Ronnie, his parents were Non-Conformists and Sargent was drawn to Quaker pacifism; for him all life was sacred and he could not contemplate killing another person. He was initially granted exemption conditional on doing work of national importance, which he found. However, the military representative appealed the decision and in due course he was arrested and handed over to the army. T. Richardson MP raised the case of Henry Sargent in the House of Commons in January 1917. However, Sargent, having refused to wear a uniform, was court-martialled and sent to Wormwood Scrubs, which he found horrendous, spending the long isolated hours remembering walks on the South Downs. A gentle, academic man, he accepted the Home Office Scheme and was in due course sent to Dartmoor.

Absolutists did not agree with those who accepted the scheme but most understood the reasons. As Bing later commented:

> although some were inclined to think, 'Well, they've let us down a bit,' I don't think there was any hostile feeling towards them. There was a recognition that we were all in the same boat, and for those with family responsibilities or whose wives were unsympathetic, it was always a terrific pressure on them ... In some cases it was necessary to save a marriage and therefore we were not critical, although those of us who were absolutists felt that ours was the right position and wished that everybody could take it.

The ability to understand and appreciate the difficulties in adopting an absolutist position was crucial to the comradeship that existed within the CO movement. There were divisions and differences of opinion but by and large there was also tolerance and solidarity. There had to be. It was no more possible for all COs to take an absolutist stand than it had been for all the women fighting for the vote in the years leading up to

1914 to take a militant suffragette position and go to prison. Finances, family pressures, exhaustion and fear all played a part. In his book *Inside the Left* Fenner Brockway, a staunch absolutist, describes how he tried to encourage a young CO, Wolstoncroft, to take the scheme because Brockway feared the young man, who came from a small village in Cheshire and had never heard of the N-CF but in Brockway's words 'had come out of a sheltered life to resist the most remorseless power on earth: the military machine', would not be able to survive prison. In fact, Wolstoncraft did not take the scheme. He suffered dreadfully in prison and was ultimately released for health reasons. Brockway considered him one of the bravest men he had ever met.

Most of the COs who went before the prison tribunal were accepted as 'genuine' and put onto the scheme. Only 100 or so were rejected as 'shirkers', which as John Graham pointed out was fairly ludicrous. Given what these men had already gone through, if they were not genuine they would probably have joined the army well before this point. Having been accepted onto the scheme, COs had to sign an undertaking that they would serve the Committee for the Employment of Conscientious Objectors with 'diligence and fidelity' on whatever work of national importance as the Committee 'may prescribe for me'; that they would live wherever they were told; and that they would follow whatever rules and regulations as to work and conduct as the Committee might make.

Dyce work camp
In August 1916 the first work camps were set up at Haverhill, in Suffolk, Newhaven in Sussex, Dyce in Scotland and Llangadock in Wales and the first released COs started work. To begin with most of the conscientious objectors were prepared to accept the difficulties, hard work, rough accommodation and very low pay which characterised the scheme. Having accepted the scheme, they wanted to make it work and were prepared to follow instructions. After the close confines of prison and the brutality of the army, they welcomed the relative freedom of working on the scheme. They were able to leave the camp and could talk and mix openly with their comrades.

Those who accepted the scheme included religious objectors, among them Quakers, Jehovah's Witnesses and political objectors ranging from socialists through to Marxists and anarchists. While some, particularly the religious conscientious objectors, were prepared to co-operate with the scheme and abide by the rules, others, among them

Marxists and anarchists, were less keen on co-operating, a stand that was not helped by the nature of the work and the often disorganised and chaotic situations that COs found themselves in. And it was not long before many COs became disillusioned.

John Brocklesby was one of 250 conscientious objectors who were sent to Dyce work camp. A small village, Dyce was about 5 or 6 miles outside Aberdeen. It was to become notorious because conditions were appalling but this was not immediately obvious. The men were housed in old army tents, which were considered unsuitable for soldiers but quite sufficient for 'conchies'. However, it was summer and according to Brocklesby: 'it was quite pleasant … and given dry weather, the tents where we slept were not too bad'. After prison life, the men appreciated the fresh air and countryside. However, once the rain arrived and autumn set in conditions became dreadful. Brocklesby recorded that 'Rain … could soon transform the camp into a quagmire and the all-pervading dampness of ground, tents, clothes and bedding could make life a burden'. 'Burden' is probably putting the case mildly: the tents were on a hillside, and as the rain poured down, the camp was effectively flooded, with water pouring through tents, drenching bedding and clothes, which were rarely dry.

The men were set to work 10-hour days in a granite quarry, digging out and 'feeding the irregular lumps into crushing machines for road repairing'. Very few of the conscientious objectors had ever done such heavy manual labour and, weakened by months in prison on a meagre diet, they found it incredibly difficult.

Despite the conditions, conscientious objectors had some freedom. According to Brocklesby's memoirs, the local people were hospitable:

> I remember no word of denigration from the local inhabitants. We were much more likely to denigrate each other – 200 men of independent and progressive thought. There were perpetual debates … in the big common room after the day's work … Quakers, Protestants of all sorts, Catholics, Communists, Atheists, Peculiar People, International Bible Students were all well represented.

With such a mix of men, there were some stormy debates. Brocklesby also mentions walking 6 miles every week to the Friends Meeting House in Aberdeen, where they were welcomed by the local Quakers and given food. He was also invited to Quaker homes.

The appalling living conditions and the work soon took their toll. According to one CO, who wrote to the N-CF: 'The weather here is wretched. The tents are all leaking … Everybody has a lot of wet clothes and no facilities for drying them. Last night when we got back to camp, our bedding and blankets were all wet … Everybody in camp has bad colds.' Around 100 men took the decision to move into a barn to escape the damp but were ordered to return to their wet tents. According to the letter writer:

> They were also ordered to do ten hours work a day at the heavy quarry work. Many of the chaps are exceedingly weak, not yet having recovered from the effects of ill-treatment. Twenty of the men who were sentenced to death in France are here … There are some who are still in a weak condition … At present our conditions are more like penalisation than exemption … We have now got two or three invalids … One case is so serious the doctor says he dare not move the patient.

The seriously ill patient was Walter Roberts. Aged 20, he had arrived at Dyce already exhausted from after four months' hard labour in prison. After two weeks working in the quarry he collapsed and died just two days later in his damp tent. Shortly before his death, he had dictated a letter to his mother, which was revealing. Telling his mother that he was dictating his letter to his comrade Bertie Wild because 'I am too weak to handle a pen myself', he told his mother not to worry 'because the doctor says I have only got a severe chill but it has reduced me very much. All the fellows here are exceedingly kind and are looking after me like bricks, so there is no reason why I should not be strong in a day or two …'.

Brocklesby recorded the death in his memoirs: 'I saw young Walter Roberts fighting a losing battle with pneumonia, brought on we were sure by sleeping in a damp bed … he should have been carried to a proper hospital … So he passed out, a true martyr to the cause of Peace and Brotherhood.' Ironically, the Home Office Scheme had created the first martyr of the CO movement, Brockway, like Brocklesby, describing Roberts as 'worthy to be the first to die in our struggle'.

Roberts' death shocked his fellow conscientious objectors, who increasingly ceased to obey orders and registered complaints about their work and conditions, which were raised in the House of Commons.

Ramsay MacDonald, who had visited Dyce, called for a more intelligent and constructive use of the men's labour but there was little public or parliamentary sympathy for the men. C.B. Stanton, MP for Merthyr, who in November spoke at a fiery meeting in Cardiff against peace activists, slammed into MacDonald saying, 'What about our sons and brothers and others who are at the front? Do they cry about a little mud in their camps?', going on to say that his own son was at the front, like others 'up to their eyebrows in mud'. Nor, as the death toll in the trenches mounted – 106,081 casualties in July 1916 alone, during the first month of the Somme offensive, was Stanton the only MP or member of the public to express their total lack of sympathy for men on the scheme.

Conditions at Dyce became impossible and by the end of October, the camp was shut down and COs were transferred to work camps or centres. Brocklesby though had determined to return to prison. In his memoirs he says that when he went to Dyce he was not an absolutist like his colleagues Murfin and Beavis but being at Dyce changed his mind. At some point two of the conscientious objectors discovered that the rocks they were digging were being used for a new road leading to a new naval aerodrome: 'I had naively assumed that this Home Office Scheme was designed to meet the scruples of men such as me; but now I was sure that the aim was to wangle us somehow into the war machine and therefore the only satisfactory attitude was the absolutist stand of Beavis, Murfin and Taylor.' Brocklesby would have taken land or hospital work; he felt it was his duty to do such service for the community but instead 'was driven to the absolute position by the Home Office Scheme'. For him there was no alternative but to go back to prison.

There was a big camp meeting to discuss the situation but at that stage Brocklesby was only supported by two other COs – Bert and Percy Larkin. The three left the camp without permission, and took a train south to see their families. They managed to get home, even though a young officer on the train thought they were spies, and were re-arrested some days later. Over the next few weeks and months many conscientious objectors were to follow Brocklesby's example, including most of the men who had been sent to France.

Princetown Work Centre, Dartmoor
With Dyce closed, conscientious objectors were sent either to other smaller camps or settlements or to Knutsford, Wakefield or Warwick

prisons, which were taken over by the Home Office Committee and turned into work centres. In the prisons, locks were taken off the cell doors, warders did not wear uniforms and conscientious objectors were allowed out in the evenings until about 9.30. COs were allowed rail passes and could elect their own committees to effectively run the camps.

Despite the relative freedoms, the nature of the work continued to be as mindless and futile as it had been at Dyce and discontent and unrest spread. Some COs, like Brocklesby, became convinced that much of the work they were doing was linked to military needs and many felt they were being put to work merely to release other men for the army. Conscientious objectors at Warwick refused to go out to work; at Llanelly men were accused of malingering and at Wakefield, men were punished for singing the 'Red Flag'. There was a ban on all forms of propaganda and nearly 100 men were sent back to prison. One of the problems was that there simply was not enough work for the growing number of men who were being brought onto the scheme.

During March 1917 many of the settlements and camps were broken up and the COs were transferred to the Princetown Work Centre at Dartmoor. Originally built to imprison French soldiers during the Napoleonic Wars, Dartmoor had subsequently become a convict settlement. Now 90 convicts were moved out and around 900–1,000 conscientious objectors – prisoners for peace – were moved in. When they first arrived Dartmoor was in a state of near chaos with little provision made for the new arrivals. No work had been organised, which meant that COs were left idle much of the time. Tensions developed when some of the more militant and politically minded men staged various protests, encouraged by news of the Russian Revolution that was breaking out. Some COs distributed political leaflets and a few walked out of a church service when the national anthem was being played. They were though in a minority.

After a while work was organised for the COs, although it was, as only to be expected, of the futile and hard labour variety.

Mark Hayler had served a first prison sentence in Wandsworth. Sent back to the army, where he was brutalised, he continued refusing orders and was court-martialled again and sentenced to one year's hard labour in Winchester. Released and re-arrested, this time he accepted the Home Office Scheme and was sent to Dartmoor:

The work we did there was worse than futile. About 200 of us were engaged on work within the prison walls, the rest were outside on the moor. I spent ten months on the moor and nearly a year on hospital work within the walls. The agricultural work was absolutely penal and organised on lines as for convicts. If we had been murderers and gangsters, the authorities could not have discovered a worse way of treating us ... the object was to *make* work. The harder it was and the more tiring it was, the better ... There was a hand roller, to which eight men were harnessed, engaged in rolling a field. I have been one of those human horses. The work we did could have been done by one man and one horse in a third of the time. And this ... in a time of the country's [food] crisis. I once worked on digging a field with about 50 others. It took us three weeks what could have been ploughed easily in one week.

Lydia Smith was one of the many women who kept the N-CF going while the committee members were in prison. She ran the publications section while Hubert Peet was in prison and wrote to the *Manchester Guardian* describing the futility of the work at and the total waste of skills that could have been put to so much better use:

There are at the Settlement between eight and nine hundred men of all shades of religious and political opinions – Quakers, Churchmen, Socialists, Plymouth Brethren, Tolstoyans, Internnationalists, and so on; their one common belief being that war is wrong. All these men have suffered imprisonment for their convictions and have been adjudged 'genuine' by a none too friendly Tribunal sitting at the prison, and have been offered this work of so-called 'national importance' on that ground. Here were men genuinely anxious to render to their country every service they conscientiously could ... What outlet did the Home Office find for the energies of these men, who are drawn from the thoughtful section of the community, whether they be doctors, accountants, University men ... or tradesmen and skilled artisans? Has the Government ... made any attempt to use the talents of these men in a way which will be most helpful to the community? The answer is unfortunately in the negative. Not only is the work futile, but the conditions under which it is performed are those most calculated to discourage the worker ... The crushing of oats is performed with antiquated machinery of the treadmill type arranged for hands instead of feet. Sixteen men are needed to work this machine and the output is six bags a day … I saw a gang of eight men harnessed to a hand-roller engaged in rolling a field … The spades, barrows, etc. are all prodigiously heavy … and all the appliances and methods are of the most antiquated nature … The coke for the gasworks and furnaces is carted by hand, teams of ten men being harnessed to a cart …

More freedom

Compared with the absolutists in prison and despite the harshness of the work, conscientious objectors at Dartmoor had some freedom and opportunity for socialising. Eric Dott, describing his time in Princetown, commented on the fact that his cell, 'which we prefer to call a room' was unlocked, the food was better than in prison, and Princetown contained a library, a games room and a gym. Objectors were able to talk openly to each other and could leave the camps for church services or Quaker meetings. They also organised social activities: debates, lectures, concerts and even plays.

Henry Sargent was also at Princetown. Unfortunately, he did not leave a personal account of his experiences but before his death he gave his companion Mrs Ronnie permission to publish information that he told her once he was dead. She wrote an account, which was published in the *Bexhill Observer* in December 1983. According to this, Sargent worked in a gang, felling trees. He was not a strong man and collapsed when carrying a heavy load. His health suffered badly at Dartmoor but there was some compensation: his fellow conscientious objectors included doctors, teachers, lawyers and actors. They produced and put on plays and organised lectures, which would have appealed to Sargent. He was also able to use his artistic skills, taking photographs of Dartmoor and producing delicate line drawings of his unlocked cell and other aspects of Princetown.

Sitting in the archives of Bexhill Museum today is a box full of memorabilia that belonged to Henry Sargent which, in the absence of diaries or letters, suggests the importance to him of his life as a CO. It contains a copy of the *C.O. Clink Chronicle*, newspaper cuttings, photographs, and a collection of programmes advertising various social events organised by COs at Princetown. One leaflet lists a winter programme of lectures such as 'Revolutionary Spirit in Modern Literature and Drama' and 'Principles of Democracy' both by C.H.

Norman and a lecture on 'Great Composers' by Harry Adkins. Also inside this fascinating box is a leaflet for a play, 'Potash & Permutter', a 'farcical comedy'. Taken all together, the contents indicate a very thoughtful man.

Cyril Heasman similarly did not leave any personal accounts of his time at Princetown, which is a shame. However, he did leave a wonderful album containing photographs, newspaper cuttings, documents relating to his tribunal and acceptance onto the Home Office Scheme, as well as song sheets and postcards. The album is a precious resource, much valued by his granddaughter and surviving family; it indicates again just how important the experience of being a CO must have been to Heasman.

Vilification and attacks

Given the appalling war casualties by 1917, it is perhaps hardly surprising that the public attitude towards conscientious objectors was extremely bitter and in April 1917 public anger was stoked up by a deliberate press campaign aimed at vilifying COs on the Home Office Scheme and at Dartmoor in particular. The *Daily Mail* spearheaded the attacks. Under inflammatory banner headlines such as '"Ha! Ha! You Can't Catch Us" Say the Dartmoor Do-Nothings', the *Daily Mail* launched a vitriolic attack on the conscientious objectors at the Princetown Work Centre, claiming that the men were living lives of relative luxury and were being 'pampered' and 'coddled'. In one issue on 23 April 1917, the *Daily Mail* displayed photographs of conscientious objectors alongside a map 'of the region across which our citizen soldiers are driving the hosts of militarism and barbarism', arguing that it was 'fitting to exhibit these typical faces of "men" who have refused to do their share of the fighting and who by their levity and idleness on Dartmoor are rousing keen resentment both on the spot and in Parliament'.

As the press campaign intensified, Sir C. Kinloch-Cooke, MP for nearby Devonport, took the campaign into the House of Commons, using every opportunity to criticise the behaviour of the Dartmoor COs, asking on 19 April 1917 whether the Prime Minister was aware that 'these cowards and shirkers attended divine service at Princetown and walked out when the National Anthem was played', and why the COs had been given Easter leave and free railway warrants when there were 'men at the front who have had no leave for two years'. Some days later on 23 April he made an apoplectic attack, saying:

I understand that from Saturday to Monday morning they are practically free for all purposes and can go away to amuse themselves. I believe, too, they keep motor cycles ... Why should they have motor cycles? Then they walk about the roads in large numbers. Why should they be allowed to go about in large numbers? ... They are provided with every possible article of clothing necessary for their work ... They work in overcoats as not to get cold, they wear woollen gloves to prevent their hands getting red, and they are given food which is as good as, if not better than, what is now given to the soldiers at the front ...

And so he went on, criticising the situation and claiming that the men were terrorising the local women. Three days later he asked that shopkeepers in Princetown should be forbidden from selling conscientious objectors any articles of food except by special permit.

'*Commander Wedgwood: How did the soldiers get to know this man was a conscientious objector?*

Sir C. Kinloch-Cooke: Because they saw him with a fishing rod.'
House of Commons, Hansard 4.4.17

On 17 May 1917 a general meeting was held at Princetown and passed a resolution, which was signed by Howard Marten, repudiating the charge of slacking and declaring that 'the men here are prepared to perform the work provided in a reasonable spirit, but protests against the penal character of the work imposed by the Home Office Committee and demands civil work of real importance with full civil right'. Ben Hyman, writing in issue 9 of the *News Sheet*, a COs' newspaper produced at Dartmoor, expressed similar views and laid the responsibility for any idleness fair and square on the Home Office Committee:

We are charged with slacking ... I emphatically give that charge the lie ... The charge of slacking (an uncultured term for lack of employment) must be laid on the proper shoulders ... All the slacking – or nearly all – that I have borne testimony to has been primarily due to the slackness of the Home Office. I say ... that if any private firm conducted their affairs in the same manner as the Home Office they would be heading straight for the services of the official receiver … We came to Princetown and found the Settlement in a state of chaos. … Topsy-turveydom reigned supreme … It was in the midst of disorder. … that the vindictive, and in all probability organised, Press campaign was launched against us …

And he continued by reiterating that the men on the Home Office Scheme were prepared to work but should be given meaningful work to do.

The damage, however, was done. Public anger reached boiling point and there were a number of vicious attacks on conscientious objectors, some of whom were now being sent out of the camps to work for private employers. On 26 April there was a public meeting at Plymouth where it was unanimously decided that conscientious objectors should be confined to inside the prison. Over the course of the next few weeks and months other attacks also took place, not just around Princetown but at other centres as well.

At Knutsford in May 1917 conscientious objectors who were working on local farms were jeered at, pulled off their bicycles, punched and kicked by a gang of local people. They were threatened with further attacks and informed the police. Needless to say, no police were in evidence when the COs cycled to work the next morning. They found an angry group waiting for them; COs were beaten up and their bicycles smashed. Hearing the noise, fifty COs came to their rescue, some arming themselves with sticks. As a consequence, ten men were arrested but when brought to court the police denied any organised attacks and the CO rescuers were blamed for causing the problem. Inflaming the situation, the police officer claimed that 'conchies' regularly jostled wounded soldiers and even claimed that one CO had hit a woman.

Similar attacks took place elsewhere. At Wakefield twelve conscientious objectors were attacked and injured and the local Friends meeting house, which provided hospitality to COs, was ransacked. Soldiers convalescing in a local military hospital attacked a group of conscientious objectors as they arrived at the Lyndhurst centre, pulling them out of the van, punching and kicking them. Their luggage was thrown into the river, as were two of the COs. Again a group of angry women attacked conscientious objectors at Lyme Regis.

Given the press attacks and public anger, conditions at Dartmoor became more punitive. The men were forbidden to visit any towns or villages except Princetown, they were not allowed to travel by train and Christmas leave was cancelled. Food rations too were dramatically reduced. A couple of newly appointed Home Office committee members, notably Majors Tyrrell and Briscoe, retired army officers, visited all the centres and insisted that regulations should be tightened up and brought in line with army discipline. Any slight infringement of rules was met by severe punishment and the return of many men to prison, not just from Dartmoor but other centres also. At Wakefield men were punished for having raised their beds slightly off the ground onto boxes and for having too many books in their cells. Punishments became so extensive that the *News Sheet* (issue 11) reported on twenty-six cases of men in Dartmoor either being fined or returned to prison or the army for offences such as leaving work because of being soaked to the skin, refusing work for principled reasons and for writing to the *Western Morning News* defending the COs' position. Many COs objected to working for outside employers, arguing that they were being used as substitutes for men who would then be forced into the army. At Wakefield the Men's Committee lodged a formal protest and 140 men, out of the 600 COs at Wakefield, pledged to resist orders; 40 of them were arrested, 7 being returned to prison as punishment.

The N-CF intervened at certain points urging men on the scheme to stop their protests, which was a strangely contradictory position to take but there was fear that protests would damage the CO movement, not a view that was welcomed by many of the men on the scheme. Probably the majority of men did accept the scheme and, despite being disillusioned, did their best to work with a shambolic and punitive system but men were not only leaving through being punished. By now men were voluntarily returning to prison, at an estimated rate of about twenty a week, preferring to join their absolutist colleagues rather than comply any further with the scheme.

Deaths
Hard work, reduced rations and punitive conditions meant that some men fell ill and there were more deaths. In February 1918 Henry Firth died at Dartmoor. He had served nine months' imprisonment in Wormwood Scrubs and Maidstone but became so ill that in November 1917 he applied for the Home Office Scheme. When he arrived at Dartmoor he was, according to the Men's Committee at Dartmoor, 'a mere bag of bones'. He was nevertheless put to work breaking rocks in the quarry. Three days later, unable to eat, he went to the doctor who

told him there was nothing wrong and sent him back to work. On subsequent visits he was told not to be selfish when thousands of other men were suffering in the trenches. Finally, he was admitted to hospital on 30 January where he was given inadequate treatment; intervention by the COs' committee led to him being given a milk diet but his condition deteriorated so alarmingly that on 6 February he died. Mark Hayler, who had by now served two prison sentences, accepted the Home Office Scheme after one years' hard labour in Winchester Prison. He was sent to Dartmoor and looked after Henry Firth:

> In Dartmoor we had one young fellow [Henry Firth] who died … He was only a boy, 21, a preacher with the Methodists. I was an orderly in the hospital and I attended him. His wife came down from Yorkshire. I can see her now sitting outside his cell near the door. He had pneumonia. He had been badly treated in Dartmoor and should never have been sent out on the moor to work in all that weather … the doctor doubted that he'd live through the night. I said, 'I'm on duty and this man is not going to die tonight.' I stayed with him all that night, and when I went off duty at 8 a.m., he was still alive. But he was not alive the next morning … All the COs followed his coffin down to the little station – they couldn't prevent this. It was put on a train at Princetown … We got to the station. It was all arranged by our own people. Some of us got hold of fog signals and put them on the line here and there. As the little train went out of the station … the signals went off, a sort of farewell. And I remember nearly a thousand men sang a hymn, 'Abide with Me'.

In protest the COs declared a day's work and hunger strike. The authorities descended and two of the organisers were handed over to the army, where they followed the usual procedure of disobeying orders, were then court-martialled and sent to prison.

The Home Office Scheme limped on until it was finally brought to an end in April 1919, when the last conscientious objectors were discharged. It had lasted for thirty-three months. Of the 4,126 conscientious objectors who had been employed on the scheme at one point or another, 27 had died and 3 had been certified insane. The government considered the scheme a success because it did reduce the numbers of COs in prison, but some conscientious objectors had mixed feelings about taking the scheme.

Chapter 8

Continuing the Struggle

'Every man you have shut away in prison for remaining true to his sense of right and wrong has gathered a courage and quiet determination'

Clifford Allen

Having voluntarily left the Home Office Scheme knowing he would be sent to prison, John Brocklesby arrived at his home where he managed to stay at liberty for six days before being arrested by 'the most gentlemanly police officer' he had ever met, one PC Kaye. Walking behind Brocklesby so passers by would not know he had been arrested, Kaye went with Brocklesby to the train station and took him to Armley Prison, where he winced on hearing that Brocklesby had been sentenced to ten years with hard labour. From Armley, Brocklesby was moved to Shrewsbury Prison where he met up with other objectors. They were chained together and taken to Wandsworth, where another thirty or so joined them, then chained in groups and taken finally to Maidstone Prison. On the way, Brocklesby reflected on how strangely his personal circumstances had changed: not so long ago he had been a respected preacher, now he was a 'criminal' in chains. At Maidstone Brocklesby was re-united with his colleagues, Beavis, Murfin and Taylor: 'the real Absolutists, which I was only becoming. In a remarkable way, I felt as if I was coming home. The high prison wall was no burden to me then, nor at any other time, for it seemed to shut out the horrible war emotions that were affecting the whole public body.'

Other conscientious objectors were also walking off the Home Office Scheme, among them Alfred Meyers, Norman Gaudie, Jack Foister, 'Corney' Barritt and Harry Stanton, who had also been in

France and who also began arriving in Maidstone. All in all about 127 men left the Home Office Scheme to join absolutists in prison around the country.

Unending cycle

By spring 1917 there were about 1,000 conscientious objectors serving time in civilian prisons, absolutists who refused to compromise with the Military Service Act. Some had been in prison since summer 1916 and had already endured one or more prison sentences. They included Clifford Allen and Fenner Brockway, chair and secretary of the N-CF, and Quakers Hubert Peet and Stephen Hobhouse. Among the absolutists were Quakers, Methodists, Anglicans and other religious objectors as well as political objectors – socialists, Marxists and anarchists. Many were members of the ILP. All were locked into what seemed like a never-ending cycle of prison, release, return to the army, court martial and return to prison once more. As soldiers in the trenches began to believe the war would never end, so too some absolutists felt they would never leave prison. The heady and optimistic moods of the early days had passed: already weakened by imprisonment, hard labour, inadequate food, isolation and monotony, the sequential prison sentences pushed objectors to their physical and mental limits, so testing their determination.

Harold Bing had served his first sentence in a military prison. He served his second sentence in the civilian prison at Winchester, where there were many COs. He believed that morale remained remarkably high, although some objectors experienced periods of depression. Time in prison tended to drag because of the monotony of imprisonment, every week being exactly the same. He managed to adapt to the drudgery:

> Possibly because I was very young I adapted myself to it. There are two attitudes on can adopt. One is feeling aggressive and resentful and hostile the whole time … [it] does have an emotionally disturbing effect. The other is to accept it and adapt to it and not worry … just take day to day as it comes without worrying about when you're going to be released.

He believed though it was harder for some men, particularly those with family responsibilities.

Mark Hayler served two prison terms firstly at Wandsworth, followed by one year's hard labour in Winchester. He took the Home Office Scheme and was sent to Dartmoor where he remained until discharged in April 1919. He considered that he coped with prison fairly well but even he had a bout of depression:

> Some could rise above it. To some prison was hell; it was really impossible for them. It didn't worry me but it worried some to such an extent that they just about went off their heads … Some people can't bear their own company, it's too much … days never end and nights never end and it's unbelievable what it can do to you and if you work yourself up into such a state, well you can bang your head against the wall, anything to change the conditions … I remember having a spell, not a long spell, of never getting out of here. If the war goes on for years, I shall be here for years and that kind of condition that is produced by thoughts like that is really astoundingly disruptive of one's character … Men would shout out in the night, anything to break the monotony. And when things went on month after month and went into years … it seemed as if there would never be an end to it.

Conscientious objectors found ways of coping with the boredom and restrictions. They swapped limited books with each other, using threads from their mailbags to lower a book to the man in the cell below and haul back his book in exchange. One conscientious objector marked out a large circle on his cell floor, took the buttons off his jacket and played tiddlywinks with the buttons: naturally he had to remove all traces of the game before the warders came into his cell in the morning. Sometimes men just withdrew into their thoughts or imagined themselves far away from their enclosed lives. Mark Hayler used to give imaginary lectures:

> I used to stand with my back to the wall and think of a subject and give a lecture on it and I wasn't there at all in the cell … I'm not psychic in any way … but I remember one morning being well away from the cell, up in Newcastle, walking in the Jesmond Dene [a wooded valley in Newcastle].

Harold Bing read as much as possible and also taught himself German and some Spanish. Pianist Frank Merrick, who spent twenty-two months in prison, kept his brain alert by practising music in his mind and 'playing' the piano on his pillow. Later he taught himself Esperanto.

One of the problems was that there was no one to talk to; speaking to other COs had to be done furtively and carried the risk of solitary confinement on a bread and water diet; Fenner Brockway endured eight months' solitary confinement for openly challenging the silence rule. Chaplains visited from time to time but most tended to poke their head round a door then scuttle away. Many disagreed with the objectors' views and made no secret of it. Harold Bing said that in Winchester 'our prison chaplain was particularly hostile and when he could abuse a prisoner when he was visiting you or preach a sermon against pacifism, he did so. Some of his sermons were bitterly against the COs.' Chaplains gave bulletins on the progress of the war during Sunday services and Bing remembered that when their chaplain had to 'announce to the whole prison population that the Armistice had been signed, he almost had tears in his eyes and in his voice because he was sorry the war had come to an end before we'd sacked Berlin. That was the sort of man he was.'

Not all prison chaplains were hostile. In his memoirs Brocklesby describes a Methodist minister who visited regularly. He asked Brocklesby what he was in for. On Brocklesby answering that his conscience would not allow him to take part in the war, the minister replied very gravely: 'It is very difficult to understand how conscience drives men in exactly opposite directions. Both my boys joined the army as a matter of conscience and one has paid with his life.' Brocklesby never forgot this reply and wrestled with it mentally for months. Later the minister told him that his second son had been killed: 'Yet never (I must emphasise this) did he by word, look or gesture, express any condemnation of my attitude.' Clearly this minister was an extraordinarily understanding man. There were others as well. The Society of Friends organised for volunteer chaplains to visit objectors. One was John Graham, who visited conscientious objectors in Strangeways Prison, Manchester, bringing news of events outside, even though it was against the rules, and seeing COs of all denominations and none.

Uncensored news

Imprisoned COs received a surprising amount of news from outside. With the cat and mouse procedure in place, COs were constantly leaving and returning to prison; they caught up with events during the brief periods outside prison and took information back into prison when they returned. As editor of the *Walton Leader*, Brockway made sure important events such as news of the Russian Revolution were included. There was one piece of news that Brockway particularly remembered:

> an exclusive story of the slaughter at Passchendaele brought in by one of our boys who had been in a guard room with a survivor. It told graphically of the ruthless, machine-like way in which the generals sent in wave after wave of thousands of men to be massacred – and all with no result. As I read it, existence seemed intolerable ... while I sat there in my cell, men were being shattered to bits.

Outside the prison the press was not allowed to publish the details; in Brockway's words: 'you had to go to prison to get uncensored news!'.

Warders, like chaplains, also varied. Many were extremely unsympathetic and harsh and lost no opportunity to inflict punishments for even the slightest infringement of rules; others were less so. Harold Bing's sister, Dorothy, remembered how warders' attitudes varied when she visited her brother:

> They let us in with a big key, the door was locked behind us and we were taken into a small room. He was brought in behind a small grille. Some warders walked a few paces away [to allow private talk] ... some were sympathetic. Harold looked so young, he looked such a boy, he was the youngest CO that was there ... some of them [warders] were hard because they had boys at the front ... When my cousin [Tom] was killed, the warden or governor came in and just blurted out 'Anyhow your cousin he's been killed in France, that's

where you should be.' It was a terrible shock for Harold, he was so fond of Tom.

Harold Bing had arrived in Winchester in January 1917, by which time he believed that the prison warders, who at first were completely confused by conscientious objectors, had become more accustomed to them and by and large 'treated us quite reasonably', although there 'were one or two who were still very bitter, very harsh, very abusive'. He personally never experienced any physical ill treatment at the hands of warders, although he did see two warders physically manhandling an objector, dragging him headfirst down the iron stairs. He believed that as time passed many of the warders softened their approach and:

> became almost sympathetic to our point of view ... Those warders who were inclined to be sympathetic always shouted at us very gruffly and harshly and then perhaps whispered a few words to us which would not be overheard ... they had to maintain a hostile front ... under that ... some became very friendly and helped us in various ways.

Responding in kind, Bing helped one warder whose daughter was having difficulty with her maths by correcting the girl's homework, which was put into his cell in secret. After the war, the warder having died, Bing and some other COs, repaying the kindnesses shown by the warder, raised money for the family and found work for the girl and her mother.

Support outside

Outside the prison walls the N-CF and other pacifist organisations continued their work of supporting COs. The N-CF's national committee kept detailed records of the whereabouts of each conscientious objector whether at a tribunal, in a guardroom, army unit or in prison. Details of these were published in the *Tribunal*, as well as information sent in by conscientious objectors themselves. N-CF members attended tribunals to give help and feed back information and arranged prison visitors in all the localities. Even when no one could gain access, N-CF members did what they could to let objectors know that friends outside were thinking of them. During Harold

Bing's first Christmas in prison, his sister and other members of the Croydon N-CF went to the prison and sang carols outside the prison walls: according to Dorothy, 'a whole bunch of us went down to Wormwood Scrubs to sing carols … it was freezing cold … the COs waved their blinds to show they had heard'. Once Harold was moved to Winchester it became much harder for the family to keep in touch.

As well as lobbying on behalf of COs and protesting their treatment, the N-CF also provided assistance to the families of conscientious objectors, who were often left all but destitute when husbands, brothers or sons were sent to prison. Harold Bing's father was chairman of the Croydon N-CF and his mother and sister kept open house, providing hospitality to N-CF members. According to Dorothy Bing: 'It became quite a social life. We met weekly, had rambles, we became quite a tight-knit group. Women were lonely, many had been ostracised … they were glad to come and bring their children to socials … it was not much fun for a little 4 or 5-year old to say "My Daddy's in prison".' At the weekly meetings, members reported on various events and read out letters they had received from CO relatives in prison. Every so often a CO who was between prison sentences would visit the meeting and bring news. Branches also collected money for CO families.

Mark Hayler was active with the N-CF before he went into prison. In his interview with the IWM, he described how: 'We had a maintenance fund, we couldn't give very much perhaps about one or two shillings a week and my mother and my sister they used to go to certain houses and pay this money … We kept a fund going and lots of other things were done to keep the homes together.' For married conscientious objectors, anxiety about the wellbeing of their families was a major concern. Hayler knew of a man living in Upper Norwood who was keen to bear witness as a CO but, being the mainstay of his family, felt he could not take that step. On Hayler saying that the N-CF would help his family, the man changed his mind and became a conscientious objector.

Harold Bing was fortunate: he had a supportive family, although initially his sister Dorothy had found it difficult to understand his decision:

I was only 14; my brother was 16½. I don't think I thought much. People said it would all be over by Christmas … as time went on and as he got older I realised the time for his call-up would come along and then I knew he would refuse it. I had a terrible mental and moral struggle. I thought this is dreadful … I felt I wished I was a boy, I would go …

After a while though she changed her views, mainly for religious reasons, and gave her brother wholehearted support: 'I could not see Jesus Christ taking up a bayonet and killing anybody so I supported him.' Dorothy and her father attended Harold's court martial and later visited him in Winchester. She remembered at the court martial that Harold was 'very wooden … the expression on his face was quite wooden, he had to put himself in a kind of shell in order to face up to it, because he's really very sensitive, my father commented on it'.

Dorothy not only attended her brother's court martial but also others: 'I went to Kingston when tribunals were taking place, taking cakes and messages to men waiting for court-martials.' She cycled to Kingston, a distance of some 20 miles. After leaving school, Dorothy went to teacher training college: 'the staff knew my brother was in prison. It had been in the local paper and tribunals were held in Croydon, everybody knew. Everyone knew that her brother was in prison.' One or two people put white feathers on her desk, which she ignored, but she was very popular and most people ignored the situation or, in one case, were supportive. As a student teacher, she was placed in her old school where she was sacked because she refused to collect for war bonds. Fortunately, a sympathetic schools inspector transferred her to a girls school and she was able to complete her training.

Harold Bing's mother found it difficult to understand his absolutist stand but nevertheless provided total support. The personal cost though was high: like many CO families, she was completely ostracised by various relatives, particularly her sisters. After the war Dorothy tried to build family bridges, but without success:

As soon as they realised Harold was not going to fight, they just cut us completely … even after the war it wasn't healed … I tried to heal the breach … [it was] terribly hateful to my mother … they just looked at me … didn't come to the funeral when she died … dreadfully hurtful. My mother was very loyal to her husband and to Harold … I was never sure how much she agreed … It had a bad effect on her.

Many conscientious objectors and members of their families were shunned or vilified by friends and relatives, which was not only painful for them but also added to the stresses on COs in prison. Hubert Peet, who served more than two years in prison, left behind a much-loved wife and three children, who missed him dreadfully. Happily, he had his wife's support and wrote lovingly crafted letters to his children, explaining exactly what he was doing and why so that they could understand his decision to be separated from them.

Family members were not always sympathetic: Hubert Peet's mother-in-law did not really understand his stand, nor were all wives as supportive as Edith Peet, or Lilla Brockway who, while her husband Fenner was in prison, lived in almost destitute conditions in a caravan with their two daughters. Harold Blake suffered in prison knowing that his wife was unhappy and felt she had been deserted. The strain of having a conscientious objector in the family could be enormous. Harold Blake's mother believed in his sincerity completely and felt everyone else should too but the fact that he was imprisoned for his views upset her dreadfully and the impact on her health shocked Blake:

> She still persisted in her faith that nobody could do aught but recognize my sincerity and act accordingly and my heart sank as I realized the crushing weight of sorrow that was in store for her. Crushing indeed it was, and its effect upon her when I again saw her after many months of incarceration … rendered me speechless and staggered me so greatly, in the weak condition in which I was then, that I was compelled to sit down in order to avoid falling …

Stepping up resistance
Many of the absolutists, having made their stand against the Military Service Act by entering prison, accepted the prison regime unless they were told to do work that they considered furthered military aims, such as producing mailbags for the navy. But as the weeks and months went by there were some who felt that resistance needed to be stepped up and work and hunger strikes took place, usually in response to unfair treatment. Some of the strikers were militants, many of whom were influenced by the Russian Revolution, news of which spread quickly through the prisons. Others, like Clifford Allen, felt that the time had come to up the ante and make a more powerful protest.

Government intransigence had turned pacifists into rebels.

In May 1917, following a third court martial and about to embark on a third prison sentence of two years' hard labour, Clifford Allen wrote to the N-CF saying that 'something more vital is needed now'. He had decided that from now on he would go on work strike, refusing to carry out any prison work. He knew it would mean severe punishment and that if he had the health and courage to carry it through, he might well spend the whole of his imprisonment in solitary confinement, subsisting for large periods of time on bread and water, forbidden to send or receive letters, have visitors or even books.

Allen wrote to Lloyd George, who had replaced Asquith as Prime Minister in December 1916, explaining why he was taking this step. For Allen, as for most conscientious objectors, the government had consistently failed to understand the position, determination and sincerity of conscientious objectors but most particularly the position of absolutists. In Allen's view the government regarded absolutists as cowards or men who 'had a mania for martyrdom', cowards because it was safer to be in prison than in the trenches and martyrs because they chose to be imprisoned. However, neither was true: the fact that absolutists had refused conditional exemption and the 'ostensibly attractive offer' of the Home Office Scheme, had endured repeated arrests, brutality in the army, courts martial and successive periods of imprisonment meant they were far from cowards. Similarly, they were not martyrs either:

> We have chosen to remain in prison ... because we cannot honestly accept anything but Absolute exemption from a Military Service Act, a form of exemption provided for in the Act ... When we say we can only accept Absolute Exemption, we mean this. As proved and admitted genuine Conscientious Objectors ... we believe War to be wrong. Thus we believe the same of Militarism, and thus we believe the same of Conscription, which is designed to equip the nation in its military and civil spheres for war ... nothing in the world will induce us to accept any compromise or enter into any bargain with a Conscription Act.

Allen wrote that despite absolutists proving that they were 'actuated by motives and opinions, which however unpopular, entitle us to be no longer classed and treated as the lowest of criminals ...' they were nevertheless being subjected to one prison sentence after another, which he stated was 'nothing less than the most deliberate persecution of genuine opinion ... Three times you have punished me for the same offence, and I believe it is my duty now to refuse to do anything in prison which would result in my acquiescing in such injustice.' He finished by warning Lloyd George that continued persecution was effectively creating centres of resistance in prison and assuring him that 'Every man you have shut away in prison for remaining true to his sense of right and wrong has gathered a courage and quiet determination.'

Although chairman of the N-CF, Allen's decision to go on work strike was personal; he always considered it should be an individual's decision and it was not N-CF policy. Although there were debates about the issue, the N-CF's national committee was opposed to strike action within the prisons. The *Tribunal* published Allen's letter on 14 June 1917 and included a piece from Dr Alfred Salter, who completely opposed strike action, arguing that 'Without occupation of some sort a man becomes a gibbering idiot', but possibly more importantly that 'dramatic action, like a work or hunger strike, will achieve nothing for our cause. The most that could be hoped for would be the compassionate release of a few individual men who had been brought near to physical and mental death. Nothing would be accomplished for the movement as a whole.' To clarify the situation the *Tribunal* published a disclaimer stating that 'Clifford Allen wishes it to be known that though he himself feels bound to refuse henceforth to do prison work ... he entirely concurs with the view of the National Committee that it would not be right to *organise* a general refusal of work in prison'.

A large number of the imprisoned absolutists, particularly religious objectors, agreed with this view. Harold Bing felt striking was counter-productive. He knew Clifford Allen, whom he considered to be 'one of the most gentle, most loving people I've ever known', and when news passed round the prison that Allen was there and had gone on work strike, 'this caused some discussion among us as to whether this was the new N-CF policy that we should none of us do prison work and whether we should follow suit'. By now Bing was working as an assistant to one of the warders and was able to visit Allen's cell and speak to him:

Clifford Allen was, for refusing to work, placed on punishment diet and put in one of the punishment cells down in the basement on bread and water … He said that 'No' this was a personal act of his and he didn't wish other people to follow his example. This puzzled me … but after thinking about it I came to the conclusion that what he meant was if anyone felt they couldn't conscientiously do prison work then they would refuse and would be able to maintain it but if they merely did it because Clifford Allen said so, they wouldn't be able to maintain it … it required a personal decision of very considerable magnitude.

As Allen's health deteriorated Bing managed to smuggle in some Horlicks tablets for him but did not agree with his action. For Bing it was a matter of tactics and in his view, ruining one's health without gaining anything did not seem very sensible. However, all movements from the peace movement through to civil rights campaign and the pre-war women's suffrage movement have included both moderate and more militant activists and the CO movement was no exception. While most of the absolutists decided against striking, some did embark on work strikes, usually to protest against what COs saw as unjust prison rules. Pianist Frank Merrick, for instance, refused to work on various occasions, once because his wedding ring was taken away.

Some COs also went on hunger strike. One of the first to do so had been the poet and printer Francis Maynell, who founded the Nonesuch Press after the war. He went before a tribunal as a conscientious objector, refused alternative service, received his call-up and, instead of waiting to be arrested, began a hunger and thirst strike before giving himself up. He was taken to the guardroom at Hounslow Barracks where he continued his strike even though he knew that he might die. Interviewed by the IWM, Maynell described how he began to have fantasies of flying to heaven and also walking home. His tongue began to dry up, which was very painful, and felt 'like a little bit of wood in the decaying barrel of my mouth, highly unpleasant'. Strangely, no one in the guardroom seemed to notice what he was doing, possibly because he handed his food to a different person each day until finally, on about the ninth or tenth day, he collapsed and was taken into a military hospital, where he was kept on his own, so as not to 'contaminate' the soldiers. He was discharged and did not go into prison.

During the early part of 1918 a number of COs went on hunger strike in various prisons: Newcastle, Maidstone, Winchester, Wandsworth,

Carlisle, Canterbury and Hull. The one in Newcastle took place in February 1918 and was a protest 'against the incompetence and inhumanity of the prison doctor'. A total of eleven conscientious objectors went on hunger strike and, like the suffragettes before them, were forcibly fed, a dreadful procedure by which a rubber tube is forced through the nose and liquid food poured through the tube. According to the men in Newcastle Prison, the same tube was used for each hunger striker, without being cleaned. The procedure was carried out brutally:

> One comrade had a disease of the nose, and suffered terrible agony through the doctor trying to force the tube up his nostril; another had a tear vein burst through the violence of the operation. All bled profusely from the nose and throat … on one occasion the doctor pulled a handful of hair out of a man's head in his anger and frequently used epithets such as 'dirty, filthy scoundrel' and the like.

In Wandsworth Prison, hunger strikers were also treated very harshly. Force feeding causes an intense thirst: to make the strikers discomfort even worse, the doctor refused the men any water and it was taken out of their cells. Milk was substituted, which was of course food. Their washing water had soap added to it so that it was impossible to drink, the result being that the men suffered from dreadful thirst after being force fed.

Force feeding led to at least one death. W.E. Burns, a belt weaver, was the first conscientious objector to go on hunger strike in Hull Prison. He had initially accepted the Home Office Scheme but, having been involved in organising a strike, was sent back to the army, disobeyed orders, was court-martialled and sentenced to two years' hard labour in November 1917. By January his health was deteriorating. He had lost weight and was finding it difficult to stand for any period of time. He asked to go back on the Home Office Scheme or to be transferred to Manchester to be closer to his family. Not receiving a response, he went on hunger strike in protest. He was force fed cocoa and milk for three days but on the fourth day the mixture went into his lungs and he choked to death.

Burns was not the only CO to die in prison. Others included Arthur Butler, who developed tuberculosis in 1917 during his third term of imprisonment. The prison doctor diagnosed influenza. His family petitioned for his release but were told that he was only slightly unwell. By December he was gravely ill. His mother arrived to see him but was refused permission to stay beyond the normal visiting time. He died the following day. Others who died included Arthur Horton, who developed pneumonia in December 1917 after fourteen months in prison; he was given cough mixture and died in January 1918; Ernest England, a Quaker from Leeds; Walter Bone; Paul Gillan and Alexander Campbell, who committed suicide. In all, at least 73 conscientious objectors died as a result of their resistance to conscription, 10 of them in prison, 24 on the Home Office Scheme, 6 in military custody and the remainder after release as a result of their weakened state.

Calls for release

As time went on most of the absolutists became increasingly weak and emaciated, not helped by the fact that in mid-1917 bread rations were halved. Many of the COs were by now also experiencing serious health problems brought on by a meagre diet, hard labour and solitary confinement. According to Harold Bing: 'Some died in prison; some went mad; some broke down in health completely and never recovered; some were discharged because they were on the point of death; some suffered terribly from insomnia.'

One whose health deteriorated was Harold Blake. He began to fear that he was losing his memory: 'I began to get apprehensive lest my memory should fail altogether, for I became aware that that faculty in me was not anything like so acute as heretofore.' To counteract this, he borrowed a copy of Shakespeare's plays from a fellow CO, Stanley Hodgson, and began to memorise them. It was hard work at first but the more he persisted, the more his memory returned to its former state. His digestive problems, however, were less easy to deal with:

It was towards the autumn of 1917 that my internal organs were becoming deranged. I suffered from spasms of extremely severe pain across my middle as though I were being screwed up in a vice. At first those spasms were separated by fairly long intervals of time, but gradually they became more and more frequent. The attack culminated in a violent turn of vomiting … I was then better until the next attack.

Blake recognised the symptoms as liver damage resulting from the poor prison diet. Ultimately, he collapsed and was taken to the prison hospital for several months.

By mid-1917 John Brocklesby, normally a large, strong man, was also becoming increasingly weak, exacerbated by reduced rations. The prison doctor refusing to take any action, Brocklesby went on an eleven-day hunger strike in protest. Clifford Allen too, who was never a strong man, was by now seriously undernourished and weak. In a letter from Liverpool Prison, Fenner Brockway wrote that one in six absolutists was now in hospital or being examined for severe loss of weight. John Graham wrote that in his experience as visiting chaplain, 'the men generally begin to find their heads fuzzy; power of concentration failed them; they read and read without understanding; their thoughts wandered ... They sometimes had not strength to walk round the yard.

The deaths and deteriorating health of the absolutists were now beginning to cause concern in the outside world and there was increasing criticism of the way they were being treated. Philip Snowden MP drew attention to their situation in the House of Commons on many occasions; during November 1917 alone he consistently asked questions about the health of a number of conscientious objectors, three of whom subsequently died. The *Manchester Guardian* described the situation of the absolutists and criticised the government's handling of absolutists and even *The Times*, not by any stretch of the imagination sympathetic to conscientious objectors, asked in an editorial on 25 October 1917 whether the punishment had not gone on long enough:

> When a man has deliberately refused to avail himself of two alternative ways of escape from prison labour; when he has, more than once, of his own deliberate choice, gone back to gaol; when he shows himself resolute to go back again and again rather than submit to that military service against which he asserts that his conscience raises for him an insuperable barrier – when he thus proves repeatedly his readiness to suffer for what he proclaims to be his beliefs, is it either justifiable or politic to go on with the punishment?

A number of influential people, not all of them sympathetic to conscientious objectors, began to question official policy and demand the release of the absolutists, or at least those whose health had seriously deteriorated and an end to repeat sentencing. Mrs Margaret Hobhouse in particular fought for the release of her son, Stephen Hobhouse, publishing a pamphlet, 'I Appeal Unto Caesar', as evidence of the urgency of the situation. The Hobhouse family being exceptionally well connected, Mrs Hobhouse's intervention carried considerable weight. Hundreds of trade-union branches, seventy local trade councils and the Labour Party protested against the continuing persecution of conscientious objectors. So too did 1,000 Anglican clergymen and 2,500 Free Church ministers who signed protests.

Faced by this barrage of criticism from influential individuals and groups, in December 1917 the government introduced some rather paltry concessions for imprisoned absolutists who had already served twelve months. These included being allowed to talk during exercise, to walk in groups, to wear their own clothes and the right to have four library books at a time. They were also allowed to employ another prisoner to clean their cells, on payment of 6*d*. Needless to say, no conscientious objectors took advantage of this. The diet remained the same, with the added problem of rations being cut and no writing materials were allowed.

At the same time the government released around 300 dangerously ill absolutists, including Stephen Hobhouse and Clifford Allen, whom many considered was within days of death. No changes however were made to the prison diet or to the conditions of hard labour. Nor was the 'cat and mouse' system ended; instead absolutists continued to be returned to their military units when their sentences ended, so ensuring they returned to prison once more after a court-martial. By March 1918 there were more than 1,100 absolutists still in prison and by October that year, there were more than 1,300 actually in prison and another 200 objectors, who had already served prison sentences, waiting to be court-martialled. It was clear that the government had no intention of accepting the validity and sincerity of the absolutists, who realised they would have to maintain their stand at least until the war ended.

Ingenious women

While many women demanded the right to be involved in war work, they were not conscripted for either industry or to join the forces as they would be during the Second World War. As a result, there were no women conscientious objectors during the First World War. However, many women played a crucial role in supporting the CO movement and in keeping both the N-CF and its journal *Tribunal* alive.

As the war continued the N-CF came under increasing official surveillance. With most of the national leadership in prison, leaving only those over military age, associate members and others stepped into their places in order to keep the Fellowship going. One was Bertrand Russell but many others were women, several of whom had been activists in the women's suffrage movement before the war. They brought with them invaluable organisational skills and considerable experience of challenging the State and of operating under police surveillance. They made a very significant contribution.

By and large women took over the day-to-day running of the Fellowship, often at considerable risk of fines and imprisonment. Catherine Marshall, member of the National Union of Women's Suffrage Societies, and a brilliant organiser, became acting honorary secretary and recruited a group of pacifist feminists to staff the national office. Largely under Catherine Marshall's direction, between 1916 and 1918, Russell produced a stream of leaflets and pamphlets, one of which led to a six-month prison sentence. Another key woman in the organisation was Lydia Smith, who ran the press section. Joan Beauchamp took over the editing and publication of the N-CF's *Tribunal*, Ada Salter organised the maintenance fund and Gladys Rinder ran the records department.

None of this was without risk. In January 1918 Bertrand Russell wrote a bitter attack on the Allied refusal of a German peace proposal made in December 1917 and criticized American policy. The article was published in the *Tribunal* and he and Joan Beauchamp were prosecuted under DORA. Russell was sentenced to six months' imprisonment, in the First Division, and Joan Beauchamp was fined £60 with costs. She refused to pay her fine and was sentenced to one month in prison. Beauchamp was persecuted again for other articles in the *Tribunal*, one of which protested the opening by French authorities of licensed brothels for British soldiers. The police raided the N-CF's offices and seized all copies of the *Tribunal* and other publications.

Despite raids, the N-CF and Lydia Smith and Joan Beauchamp kept the *Tribunal* going throughout the war, even though its circulation dropped substantially. They took the precaution of editing the *Tribunal* anonymously with only Joan Beauchamp's name appearing as publisher. Anticipating raids, a sympathetic printer, Howell Street, offered to print the journal at his small printing press in Streatham. However, following the publication of a poster headed 'Stop the War', police raided this premises and smashed the printing machinery, removing books, leaflets and invoices. That night police called on Joan Beauchamp insisting they tell her the name of the *Tribunal*'s editor, which she refused to do. Despite ransacking her office, the police failed to unearth Lydia Smith's name.

Now under constant surveillance, Lydia Smith and Joan Beauchamp continued to keep the paper going, using a small hand press bought by the N-CF and secretly installed in the back room of a house in London. Getting copy to the printers as well as collecting and distributing issues posed considerable problems, but being highly ingenious women, they came up with a number of very successful ruses. On at least one occasion, proofs were smuggled out of the N-CF offices hidden in a baby's shawl, an elderly woman carrying the baby and having apparently visited the office for financial help. On other occasions, copies of the *Tribunal* were smuggled out from six different premises. One of the most extraordinary near misses is described in the N-CF Souvenir, which was published after the war, and describes how a 15-year-old messenger boy collected copies of the *Tribunal* from the offices but, because they were too heavy for him to carry, left them on the Thames Embankment, in charge of a policeman. Clearly N-CF staff were highly alarmed but apparently the policeman had no idea what he was guarding and the copies were retrieved safely. The police were never able to establish the name of the editor so focused their attention on Joan Beauchamp who by now was listed as both printer and publisher. She was ultimately fined £200 with 25 guineas costs, a very hefty sum of money, or fifty-one days' imprisonment. She appealed and the case dragged on until January 1920, when she was finally sentenced to twenty-one days' imprisonment. She was released after eight days, the very last edition of the *Tribunal* on 8 January 1920 carrying a report of her dedicated work in keeping the journal going.

Chapter 9

Release and Aftermath

'We … made a pledge to resist conscription and the military power … We have survived the test.'

Clifford Allen

As strikes continued in the prisons and pressure mounted for the release of conscientious objectors, the government made a final attempt to solve the problem of the absolutists without actually releasing them. The idea was to move absolutists to a special centre, where they would do prison work in conditions of relative freedom, while still being prisoners. No doubt the government thought this was an excellent scheme; in the event it demonstrated yet again how little they understood the absolutists' stand.

In September 1918, groups of absolutists who had already served two years or more were moved out of various prisons and transferred to Wakefield Prison. Cell doors were kept unlocked; the men could wear their own clothes, mix freely and were given various privileges in terms of prison visits and letters. However, like all the other schemes, this one backfired. When the men arrived at Wakefield, nothing had been organised for them. They formed their own committee, organised their own food and cleaning rotas and, when the Home Office finally announced some sort of work programme, the men refused to co-operate in any way. The committee, which included Walter Ayles and Scott Duckers, issued a statement, the fourth point in the manifesto stating:

It appears the Government still misunderstand our principles, in that they take for granted that any safe or easy conditions can meet the imperative demands of our conscience. No offer of schemes or concessions can do this. We stand for the inviolable rights of conscience in the affairs of life. We ask for liberty to serve, and if necessary to suffer, for the community and its well-being. As long as the Government denies us this right, we can only take with cheerfulness and unmistakeable determination whatever penalties are imposed upon us. We want no concessions. We desire only the liberty to serve.

The N-CF circulated thousands of copies of the Wakefield manifesto and the men were returned to their prisons to continue their sentences and their stand. It was the last scheme the government tried and it had failed.

End of hostilities

Finally, on 11 November 1918, the fighting ended and the guns fell silent. In terms of hostilities the First World War was over, although the Paris peace conference would not take place until 1919. In Britain alone more than 3 million men were dead, wounded or missing in what was the bloodiest war ever known. In all the warring countries there was hardly a family who had not lost a brother, son, husband or uncle.

Incarcerated in various prisons, conscientious objectors heard the news, which they had been expecting for a while. Fred Murfin, Norman Gaudie and John Brocklesby were working in the tailor workshop in Maidstone Prison, patching shirts and machining uppers to leather shoes. Brocklesby described their reactions: 'Then on the eleventh day of the eleventh month at the eleventh hour suddenly all the buzzers in Maidstone began hooting and we could hear far away frantic cheering. Fred was working at a table about two yards from me and he smiled across and uttered a fervent "Thank God!"'

Sitting in his punishment cell, Fenner Brockway, who had learned to tell the time by watching the sun's shadow creep along his cell wall, waited for the sun to reach a crack in the wall, which he estimated would be 11 o'clock. It did. Nothing. Then he heard the sound of the hooters outside and broke down.

It was however to be five or more months before Brockway, Brocklesby and their comrades were released. The end of hostilities did not mean the end of prison for the absolutists, or for their colleagues in Home Office centres and the NCC.

Riots continue

There were more than 1,000 absolutists in prison and others were still going through the cycle of discharge and re-arrest. Hardly surprisingly, some absolutists had reached the end of their tether, and an unprecedented rebellion broke out in Wandsworth Prison. Trouble had begun in October 1918, a few weeks before the Armistice was signed, when some twenty COs went on hunger strike but, not surprisingly, tensions increased after 11 November when it became clear that, despite petitions from influential people, conscientious objectors would not be released from prison until serving soldiers had been demobbed. No doubt the public would have been infuriated if they had been but the delay sparked off a wave of hunger strikes; forcible feeding continued, some COs being temporarily released under the cat and mouse act, then being re-arrested and imprisoned once their health had improved.

At Wandsworth socialist and anarchist COs, infuriated by the delay in release, and led by flamboyant anarchist Guy Aldred, stepped up their protests and a full-scale riot broke out. Other much smaller demonstrations occurred in Leicester, Leeds, Pentonville, Liverpool, Newcastle and Preston prisons but the largest by far was at Wandsworth, which included a civilian wing and a military wing, where 108 conscientious objectors were housed. Not all of them were militants.

Rioting took the form of speaking openly, refusing prison work, making political speeches and refusing to come in from exercises. Protestors sang the 'Red Flag' and 'The International' and threatened to break furniture unless they were released. Authorities responded alternately with offers of concessions and brutal punishments, neither of which worked. According to one CO, E.H. Ellison: 'They continued striking … We then asked for books, letters and visitors (these were all stopped) but were refused. We then refused to come in from exercises … Officers drew batons and got excited … We had our little concerts through the window, and a little tin-rattling and door banging.'

Those who had taken part were put into punishment cells in the basement. The cells had not been used for years and were damp and filthy. From within the cells, the objectors continued their protest, shouting through the windows and breaking up furniture. The leaders were put on the bread and water punishment diet but threw the bread out of the window. Finally, after a week's hunger strike Guy Aldred and nineteen other militants were temporarily released under the cat and mouse procedure.

The wider CO movement did not support the actions, although no doubt understood the reasons. Quaker COs at Wandsworth refused to join the protest and the N-CF, which reported on the events in the *Tribunal*, made no comment. Unfortunately, matters did not end here. One of the COs who had refused to take part in the rebellion was mocked by the chief warder, who accused him of accepting privileges and being too frightened to join the rebels. In reaction the CO smashed up his cell and went on hunger strike. In a sworn statement, which was published anonymously in the *Tribunal* on 23 January 1919, the CO described how he was treated:

> Two warders entered the cell and pushed me outside onto the landing rails, where I was seized by five others. I was then frogmarched along the landing, being kneed in the back at every few steps … by an officer … who was also half strangling me, and punched in the back of my head by another … we arrived at a flight of steps … an attempt was made to hurl me headlong, but managing to grab a rail I averted this … Arriving in punishment cell … I was placed in a body-belt and left till teatime, when one hand was released to enable me to eat my tea. This I refused to do … About 10am … I was taken before the medical officer, who informed me that I was a lunatic, and … should be treated as such. I was then taken to a padded room and placed in a strait-jacket … at dinner time … I again refused to take any food, but asked to be allowed to make water … I was told I must wait … it was not till nearly 3pm that an officer brought a convict to me for this purpose. By this time I was experiencing much pain from the strait-jacket which … appeared to me to be strapped much too tight … preventing me from breathing freely. The convict … was to hold a chamber to me and do those things … which, my hands being confined, I was unable to do myself. Under these circumstances, I found it impossible to ease myself …

The CO was kept in the strait jacket until the evening, the doctor refusing to loosen the straps or allow him to use the lavatory. The CO was in considerable pain and discomfort, on one occasion vomiting from pain. During the evening the strait jacket was taken off for ¾ hour, then replaced. In all, the CO was kept constrained in this way for 24 hours before the jacket was finally taken off. After hunger striking for seven days, he was temporarily released under the cat and mouse procedure.

In February 1919 a new governor was appointed at Wandsworth to stamp out the Wandsworth rebellion; describing the COs as 'damned mutinous swine', he ruthlessly attempted to enforce discipline, which eventually led to a official inquiry. Nor did his attempts prevent protests, which rumbled on until the COs were finally released.

Release

Outside prison trade unions and others continued to press for COs to be released. Winston Churchill had become Secretary of State for War and he, together with the War Office, was keen to be rid of the problem. There were objections within government and from the press but finally on 3 April 1919 it was decided to begin the process of release. Given the way the government had dealt with COs during the war, it is not surprising that the process of release was fairly chaotic, and the final batch of absolutists was not released until August 1919. And even until the end COs were being handed over to the army and court-martialled because conscription did not finally end until 1920. The Home Office work camps were closed down in April, releasing men who had taken the scheme and in 1920 the NCC ended, releasing those objectors.

John Brocklesby recorded his release from prison:

we were released as a result of pressure from the Railwaymen's Union who pled our cause … April 12th 1919 was our day of liberation, to the great annoyance of those who were still waiting to see their boys demobbed from the army … I was on my best prison job, sewing for the first (and last) time the uppers of a pair of 'civvy' shoes … 'Brocklesby, Gaudie, Murfin wanted!' called out the Assistant Governor … I couldn't believe we were going out and I did want to finish those shoes. 'I'll come back and finish these,' I said. But I never did. We were taken to our cells to gather our personal possessions … and as we marched back up A Hall the men were standing at their doors waiting the order to proceed to work. They saw us 'on our way out' and a low muffled cheer began, swelling high and rolling along that house of pain. It was against all the rules, and I doubt if such a thing ever happened before or since. It gripped my heart and almost made me weep.

Fenner Brockway was also released in April 1919, having been in prison for twenty-eight months. He caught the earliest train to London, so stunned by his freedom that 'I could not take in the scenes and persons about me.' However, for him, as for the others, there was a final extraordinary communication from the army:

The *finale* of my war-time experiences came a few weeks later. The postman brought a buff envelope with 'On His Majesty's Service' printed bold and black. Inside was a form from the War Office recording that I had been discharged from the Army and stating that my behaviour had been so bad that if I ever attempted to join the Army again I would be subject to a term of two years' imprisonment with hard labour.

Clearly, the War Office had no sense of humour or irony.

Discrimination
After three-and-a-half years all conscientious objectors were now free men but settling back into post-war life was not always easy and the consequences of imprisonment and conscientious objection continued for some while. In 1917 when the Representation of the People Bill, which would give the first group of women the right to vote, was passing through Parliament it included a rather vindictive sub-clause by which conscientious objectors who had been exempted from military service or who had been court-martialled – that is, all COs apart from those in the NCC – would be disqualified from voting in local or national elections for five years from the end of the war. Despite powerful objections put forward by men such as Lord Hugh Cecil, who argued that:

it is the very essence of the conscientious objector's position that he says that the State has, up to a point, undoubtedly authority over him, but that in this respect he is bound to obey a higher law … We can only say their conscience is mistaken … but are you going to disqualify people and punish them for being mistaken in their opinions? If you do you are surely back again to the old familiar ground of religious persecution …

Of course, this was exactly what the government had done, and the clause remained in the Act of 1918. Given the war was not technically over until August 1921, this meant that COs were unable to vote until August 1926.

For most COs though, this was the least of their worries. Poor health, financial hardship and difficulties in finding a job were far more pressing concerns. Most COs came out of prison in extremely poor health. Some, including Clifford Allen, who left prison weighing only 8 stone (112lb) and lost one lung as a result of tuberculosis contracted in prison, never recovered full health. Families too had suffered great hardship – Fenner Brockway often considered that their wives had a much harder time than those who were in prison; they had to live in a 'war-mad world' and deal with the social ostracism caused by being married to conscientious objectors.

Prejudice against conscientious objectors remained widespread even after the war had ended, which made finding a job very difficult. John Brocklesby's family welcomed him home but he was,

> surprised to find how bitter local feeling was against me; it seemed much worse than in 1916. I had thought that having proved myself sincere they would give me credit for it. But no! They had suffered the poisoning effects of nearly three more years of war … I had beaten the military and they hated me for it. I could feel it as I walked in the streets, and I saw it in the faces of people who at one time pretended to be friends.

His first job, as a teacher at the Yorkshire School for the Deaf, lasted only one week; it ended once the staff knew he had been a CO. Subsequently, he found work in Durham, met up with Maurice Rowntree and went to Vienna to work with the Friends War Victims Relief.

Mark Hayler too suffered from having been a CO in prison:

> It's dogged me all my life … I wished it hadn't been so. Even when I became a director of the building society years afterwards, I was asked to go on the television, and the directors of the building society saw it in *Radio Times* … they never knew what my views were of course. I said, 'You won't want to be friends with me after you know what my story is.' … they said, 'No, it won't make any

difference.' … they just laughed, but I was surprised what the reaction was, very friendly but it was still there, they would have preferred if I had resigned from the board.

Immediately after the war, Hayler applied for a number of very good jobs but when he went to interview: 'When they knew I'd been a CO that was the end. The final question was always, "What did you do in the Great War?" No one would be responsible for employing a man who had been in prison. I wish it hadn't been so … I spent two years in Dartmoor. You've been tainted.'

Henry Sargent did not tell anyone about his time as a CO. In terms of work, he was more fortunate than some. Released before Armistice Day, because of poor health, he went first to London and then through a friendship with the Revd J.C. Thompson, who had set up Bexhill Museum, went to Bexhill as Thompson's assistant curator. In 1924 he became curator of the museum, a position he held until his death in 1983. As curator he built up the museum's natural history collection and became well known for his lectures, illustrated with his own drawings that are still on display in the Sargent Collection, named after him. No one other than close family knew he had been a CO until after his death. Perhaps he feared that the good folks of Bexhill would have been shocked to know that their highly respected and respectable curator had been in Dartmoor.

Many employers refused to employ conscientious objectors; some job advertisements specifically stating that COs need not apply. When the war finished, David Thomas moved to Bangor where very few people knew him and although he had taught in schools, began studying for an MA, hoping to get a job as a tutor in adult education. According to his son,

He wanted to teach and but he wanted to teach grown-ups. But there wasn't a chance at all of becoming a tutor in adult education without a degree … but he never did get a full-time appointment. He became a part-timer with evening classes but he never succeeded in getting a post as a lecturer or as a tutor and he did mention that he suspected it was because of his background as a conscientious objector. There were one or two on the appointments panel who were opposed to his conscientious objector stand.

Eventually though, David Thomas achieved a lifelong ambition and became a part-time tutor with the Workers Education Association.

Harold Bing's sight was permanently affected by years of sewing mailbags in prison. When he was finally released from prison, he returned home to Croydon for the first time in thirteen months. He wanted to teach but soon found that discrimination against COs was rife: 'After the war, if you looked through the advertisement pages of, say, the *Times Educational Supplement* where you get all the jobs advertised, very frequently at the head of the advert was, 'No conscientious objector need apply.' Advert after advert said that.' Eventually, a sympathetic headmaster offered him a job.

Fred Murfin received a warm welcome from nearly everyone when he returned home to Louth, Lincolnshire, where his parents lived:

> I didn't meet with any cold shoulders, but plenty of friendship. I knew everybody at the Chapel my parents attended; for years I had taught in the Sunday School, so I went the next Sunday. The mother of one of my playmates said she was pleased to see me home – but she wouldn't shake hands with me. The Minister came to welcome me home, though I'd never met him before.

Fortunately too, his previous employer found a job for him in a London printing firm, doing the work he had done before the war.

The final conference
With the war over, the N-CF was uncertain about its future. Some wanted the Fellowship to become a strictly pacifist organisation, socialist members wanted it to become a revolutionary organisation while others wanted the N-CF effectively to return to its anti-conscription origins working to ensure that conscription would not be re-introduced. In the end, following many heated debates, Fenner Brockway and Clifford Allen decided that the N-CF should be closed down and replaced by various specialist committees, each of which could pursue particular aspects of the CO and anti-war movement.

The N-CF held its final conference on 29 and 30 November 1919 at Devonshire House, in London. Some 400 delegates from branches all over the country attended; most of them had been in prison. Fenner Brockway moved the National Committee's resolution, which proposed the formation of a committee to set up a new organisation.

Clifford Allen, looking worn and emaciated and much older than his 30 years, gave the final address. Other speakers included Ramsay MacDonald and George Lansbury. Bertrand Russell and Philip Snowden, who had worked tirelessly for COs in the House of Commons, were also present. Delegates stood in silence as the names of the COs who had died in the struggle were read out.

Brockway's resolution was hotly debated and there was much opposition but in the end by 244 votes to 171 the N-CF voted itself out of existence. In his final address, Clifford Allen spoke movingly of how the N-CF had formed, what its aims had been, how much they had suffered but how much they had achieved. It was, according to those who were present, an extraordinarily moving speech. Those who heard it, never forgot it.

> Three years ago there assembled in this hall a very notable gathering. It represented men who held every variety of religious and political opinion. We were on the eve of a memorable experience ... We stood here and made a pledge. That pledge was to resist conscription and the military power. Today we reassemble. We have survived the test, and I suggest to you that that fact is in itself of very great significance.

Allen went on to say that the test had involved great suffering but that they should not compare their suffering with 'the anguish of those who have died and been mutilated in the war ... many of them are dead, but we still have the opportunities of life before us ...'. Looking back to 1916, he described how the

> human race was in the grip of contrary instincts. On the one hand were bitterness, hatred and terror ... On the other hand you had from countless individuals ... the most wonderful exhibition of self-sacrifice and unselfish heroism ... Above all things, men were held by a world spell, and that was the spell of the military machine. Fearless men, keen-minded men, gentle men, believed it their duty to bow before that machine ... We ... were called upon to become part of this world adventure ... It is not possible ... to estimate the mental and spiritual struggle of facing that challenge unless they have in fact been potential conscripts ...

It matters not whether we were in the Non-Combatant Corps, refusing to bear arms, whether we took alternative service, whether we became part of the Home Office Scheme, or whether we were absolutist and remained in prison – all of us shattered the infallibility of militarism. That … is a mighty achievement … We are proud to have broken the power of the military authority … We have defeated it; we will defeat it again if conscription should be continued …

Allen called upon the conference to look to the future and take responsibility for helping to build a new socially responsible world, saying 'we have a chance now to take no small part in rebuilding constructive hope in the world', and he concluded his address by saying:

There have been some times when I wondered if the struggle was worth while. But the certainty of hope for me is this. It was not some outworn isolated creed that we cherished. We have discovered in our prison cells that very notion which is today challenging the old world order – the notion that men will only feel obliged to serve the community … when they have come to respect each other's liberty. We were in prison – today we are free. But the world is still in prison. It can be released by the spirit of unconquerable love. 'Ye that have escaped the sword, stand not still'.

The legacy
COs did not stand still. Many of them continued working for peace for the rest of their lives. Several, including Harold Bing, Fenner Brockway and Herbert Runham Brown played a major role in the peace movement that emerged from 1919 and which would flourish right up to the outbreak of the second global conflict in 1939.

Immediately after the war Fenner Brockway, who remained a socialist and anti-war activist throughout his long life, worked for prison reform with Stephen Hobhouse and was co-founder and chair of the No More War Movement, which was launched in 1921. From 1926 he worked closely with War Resisters' International and once the Second World War arrived, though no longer an absolutist pacifist, chaired the Central Board for Conscientious Objectors, which was formed in 1939 to help the second generation of conscientious objectors. His anti-war activism did not end there; in 1958 together with Bertrand Russell, Victor Gollancz, Michael Foot and others he was one of the founder members of the Campaign for Nuclear Disarmament (CND).

Richard Porteous and Harold and Dorothy Bing also continued working for peace; like Brockway, they were closely involved with the No More War Movement, and during the 1920s Richard Porteous' sister Margaret worked with Harold Bing in setting up the British Federation of Youth with the ultimate aim of creating an international youth movement that 'work for Peace through mutual understanding'.

John Brocklesby too continued as a peace activist right up to his death; a photograph in the *Scunthorpe Telegraph* of August 1962 shows 'Old Brock' carrying out a 'vigil for peace' beside the war memorial in Oswald Road, Scunthorpe in memory of the thousands of people who died when the first atom bomb was dropped on Hiroshima. He died four months later, aged 73.

Others too promoted peace and social justice. Following both the First and Second World Wars, Corder Catchpool worked with other Quakers to help war victims in Germany. During the early 1930s, in Germany, he defied anti-Jewish laws and visited Jewish prisoners, seeing first-hand the disturbing signs of the early concentration camps. During the Second World War, he supported COs in Britain and protested against the Allied mass bombing of Germany.

Not only did many of the First World War conscientious objectors take key roles in the inter-war peace movement but also they helped to inspire and even create the next generation of pacifists and conscientious objectors, laying the basis for a peace movement in Britain that continues to this day. Naomi Rumball, speaking of her grandfather Cyril Heasman, said, 'He must have had an enormous influence. I've always felt quite proud of him; in my family it would have been thought to be a brave stance that he took.' Naomi never met him; Cyril died when her mother Alma was only 13. However, her mother Alma, Cyril's daughter, was a lifelong pacifist and during the Second World War went to Horton-cum-Beckering, a pacifist commune where many COs worked on the land. Alma also married a man who likewise became a conscientious objector during the Second World War.

Lasting achievements
There were only 16,000 conscientious objectors during the First World War, a miniscule number compared with the millions of men who

enlisted and fought. However, their impact was enormous. As Clifford Allen described, they managed to defy the military machine and the law of the land by refusing to be conscripted and by refusing to pick up arms and kill their fellow men at a time when legislation insisted that they did so. By and large peaceful and generally law-abiding men, they chose to break the law, no matter what the consequences were – and these ranged from social ostracism through to imprisonment and the possibility of a death sentence, albeit not carried out. By their actions, they proved that it was possible to defy the State, using almost entirely passive resistance. On grounds of deeply held conscience, they refused to co-operate with a State that they believed was making the wrong decisions.

First World War conscientious objectors were trailblazers. By their courage and determination, they established the right of conscientious objection. As George Dutch stated in an interview with the IWM:

> we proved that any decent modern government could not coerce man's conscience … We were nothing but sand in the machine, sources of dissatisfaction really … it was utter folly to put us in the army and we proved that. Also, we set the notion of conscientious objection really going. There's no doubt that in any future war, small or large, you'll have conscientious objectors … We started a movement which means that no war can be fought in the future without conscientious objection coming up.

When war and conscription returned once more twenty years later, provisions for COs were far more humane than they had been in the First World War, something that Harold Bing recognised: 'The National Service Acts were more generously drafted, the tribunals were more carefully appointed and there was no military representative on them … the hearings were all, I think, much fairer …'. There can be no doubt that the courage of the First World War conscientious objectors and the fact that they had been prepared to endure brutality, ostracism, long terms of imprisonment and even face death ensured that during the Second World War the right of conscientious objection was far more firmly established and far better provided for. The government during that war knew that it would be foolish to coerce men into the forces as had been done during the First World War. Official treatment of Second

World War conscientious objectors was certainly more tolerant and humane than it had been twenty years before.

More than 60,000 men and some 1,000 women took their stand as conscientious objectors in Britain during the Second World War. When they came to make their decisions and to take their stand many of them said they owed a huge debt of gratitude to the courage and example of the conscientious objectors who had gone before them.

Bibliography and Further Reading

Beckett, Ian, *Home Front 1914–1918: How Britain Survived the Great War*, The National Archives, 2006

Bell, Julian (ed.), *We Did Not Fight: 1914–19 Experiences of War Resisters*, Cobden-Sanderson, 1935

Boulton, David, *Objection Overruled*, MacGibbon & Kee Ltd, 1967

Braithwaite, Constance, *Conscientious Objection to Compulsions Under the Law*, William Sessions Ltd, 1995

Brock, Peter, *'These Strange Criminals': An Anthology of Prison Memoirs by Conscientious Objectors from the Great War to the Cold War*, University of Toronto Press, 2004

Brock, Peter and Young, Nigel, *Pacifism in the Twentieth Century*, Syracuse University Press, 1999

Brockway, Fenner, *Inside the Left*, first published George Allen & Unwin, 1942, repr. Spokesman, 2010

Catchpool, Corder, *On Two Fronts: Letters of a Conscientious Objector*, first published 1918, 3rd edn George Allen & Unwin Ltd, 1940

Central Board for Conscientious Objectors, *Troublesome People: A Reprint of the No-Conscription Fellowship Souvenir: describing its work during the years 1914–1919*, originally published by the N-CF as the N-CF souvenir, 1919, Central Board of Conscientious Objectors, 1940

Chamberlain, W.J., *A C.O. in Prison*, No-Conscription Fellowship, 1916

Ellsworth-Jones, Will, *We Will Not Fight ...*, Aurum Press, 2008

Goodall, Felicity, *A Question of Conscience: Conscientious Objection in the Two World Wars*, Sutton Publishing, 1997

Graham, John W., *Conscription and Conscience: A History 1916–1919*, first published George Allen & Unwin Ltd, 1922, repr. Augustus M. Kelly, 1969

Hayes, Denis, *Conscription Conflict*, Sheppard Press, 1949

Hobhouse, Mrs Henry, *'I Appeal Unto Caesar': The Case of the Conscientious Objector*, George Allen & Unwin Ltd, 1917

Morehead, Caroline, *Troublesome People: Enemies of War 1916–1986*, Hamish Hamilton Ltd, 1987

Peace Pledge Union, *Refusing to Kill: Conscientious Objection and Human Rights in the First World War*, Peace Pledge Union, 2006

Rae, John, *Conscience and Politics: The British Government and the Conscientious Objector to Military Service 1916–1919*, Oxford University Press, 1970

Russell, Bertrand, *The Autobiography of Bertrand Russell 1914–1944* (Vol. 11), George Allen & Unwin Ltd, 1968

Smith, Lyn, *Voices Against War: A Century of Protest*, Mainstream Publishing Company Ltd, 2009 (in association with the IWM)

Walker, Joyce A., *A Cloak of Conscience? Dyce Work Camp, Conscientious Objectors and the Public of NE Scotland, 1916*, 2011

Unpublished memoirs
Brocklesby, John, 'Escape from Paganism'
Murfin, Fred, 'Prisoners for Peace'

Newspapers, periodicals and archives
Hansard, 1913–19
Labour Leader
The Times Digital Archive, 1785–2007
Tribunal

Voices

Imperial War Museum Sound Archives
Extracts have been taken from the following IWM sound archives, which are housed in the IWM, London. The name of the person quoted is followed by the IWM catalogue number and date of interview (in brackets).

Bing, Dorothy: 555 (1974)
Bing, Harold: 358 (1974)
Brockway, Fenner: 478 (1974)
Dutch, George: 356 (1974)
Evans, Alfred: 489 (1974)
Hayler, Mark: 357 (1974)
Littleboy, Wilfred: 485 (1974)
Marten, Howard: 383 (1974)
Maynell, Francis: 333 (1974)
Merrick, Frank: 381 (1974)
Winsten, Stephen: 784 (1976)

Recollections
Heasman, Cyril: interview with Naomi Rumball, granddaughter
Porteous, Richard: interview with Felicia Shannon, niece
Sargent, Henry: interview with Margaret Shannon, niece by marriage
Thomas, David: interview with Angharad Tomos, granddaughter

Index